The Coaching Relationship in Practice

April 2016

Lucas,

I've just started reading your book, 'Management, Information and Power' and excited as it seems to be the first sustained application I've seen of a Heideggerian approach to a vital subject.

I'm hoping we may get to have the opportunity to delve deeper into subjects of shared interest!

Best wishes

Geoff

SAGE was founded in 1965 by Sara Miller McCune to support the dissemination of usable knowledge by publishing innovative and high-quality research and teaching content. Today, we publish more than 850 journals, including those of more than 300 learned societies, more than 800 new books per year, and a growing range of library products including archives, data, case studies, reports, and video. SAGE remains majority-owned by our founder, and after Sara's lifetime will become owned by a charitable trust that secures our continued independence.

Los Angeles | London | New Delhi | Singapore | Washington DC

The Coaching Relationship in Practice

Geoff Pelham

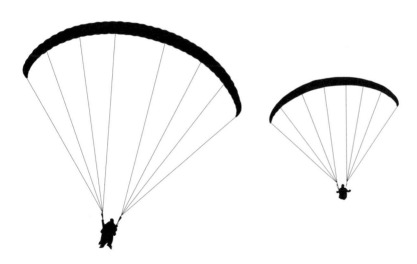

Los Angeles | London | New Delhi
Singapore | Washington DC

Los Angeles | London | New Delhi
Singapore | Washington DC

SAGE Publications Ltd
1 Oliver's Yard
55 City Road
London EC1Y 1SP

SAGE Publications Inc.
2455 Teller Road
Thousand Oaks, California 91320

SAGE Publications India Pvt Ltd
B 1/I 1 Mohan Cooperative Industrial Area
Mathura Road
New Delhi 110 044

SAGE Publications Asia-Pacific Pte Ltd
3 Church Street
#10-04 Samsung Hub
Singapore 049483

Editor: Susannah Trefgarne
Assistant editor: Laura Walmsley
Production editor: Rachel Burrows
Marketing manager: Camille Richmond
Cover design: Wendy Scott
Typeset by: C&M Digitals (P) Ltd, Chennai, India
Printed and bound by CPI Group (UK) Ltd,
Croydon, CR0 4YY

© Geoff Pelham 2016

First published 2016

Library of Congress Control Number: 2015933639

British Library Cataloguing in Publication data

A catalogue record for this book is available from
the British Library

MIX
Paper from
responsible sources
FSC® C013604

ISBN 978-1-4462-7511-5
ISBN 978-1-4462-7512-2 (pbk)

At SAGE we take sustainability seriously. Most of our products are printed in the UK using FSC papers and boards.
When we print overseas we ensure sustainable papers are used as measured by the Egmont grading system.
We undertake an annual audit to monitor our sustainability.

Contents

About the Author

Dr Geoff Pelham (MBACP Reg, MA Business and Executive Coaching) is Director of Supervision at PB Coaching, based in Leeds. He is an executive coach and coach supervisor working with people in the public, private and not-for-profit sectors. He is also an accredited psychotherapist. His practice is rooted in relational and existential approaches to therapy and coaching. This background leads to an abiding interest in the psychological dimension of coaching and the possibilities of practitioners developing the capability to work more deeply and effectively with the emotional and relational aspects of coaching.

He is particularly involved with the education and training of coaches, delivering Postgraduate, EMCC-accredited programmes in the UK and also at Michael Smurfit Business School, University College Dublin (UCD) in Ireland. In addition to working with individuals he is involved with organisations seeking to introduce and sustain coaching cultures, including the establishment of internal coaching and supervision capability, the challenges facing internal coaches, and the mindset and skills required for managers taking a coaching approach.

Geoff's PhD was in the area of the philosophy of science as applied to the behavioural sciences, and it is from this background that he is interested in, and often critical of, the evidence-based approach to coaching. For the past decade he has been exploring Heideggerian and existential approaches, and is particularly interested in the personal and cultural as a relational field; for example, of mood as a field which is personal but not just personal.

Acknowledgements

I would like to thank my partner Jenny Stacey, for her constant support and from whom I have learned so much about relationships. Similarly to my 'children', now young adults, Kathryn, Sarah and Jon, who make life special.

I'd also like to thank colleagues at PB Coaching, whose encouragement has made it possible for me to write this book, and who have been a constant source of support and conversation about the idea I've written about here. Particular thanks to Colm Murphy and Yvonne Fagan and colleagues at UCD, from whom I've learned so much.

Special mention for my 'writing coach' Andrea Perry, who helped me find the 'voice' I wanted for the book, and who both encouraged and challenged me in the style and content of what I've written.

Thanks also to Peter Bluckert, who embodies the gestalt approach, for the many, many conversations in the pub digging deeply into the subjects covered in this book.

Introduction

As its title suggests, this book is about: relationships, which are at the very heart of coaching; our relationships with coachees and others involved in the coaching process; and how we bring ourselves into the coaching relationship. I am keen to write the book and also daunted, because we will be touching on fundamental questions that will challenge us as coaches and also, more profoundly, challenge us in our very 'being'; in how we are as people and the manner in which we live our lives.

'Relationship' is the key term, but it is hard to define. Dictionaries don't help much; for example, relationship can be defined as 'the way two or more people or things are connected' (Pearsall 1999). This is perfectly understandable, but both too formal and kind of mechanical to catch what we are getting at. To get a sense of what we are trying to grasp, bring to mind someone who has profoundly affected your life in a negative way, maybe a parent, a teacher, a doctor, a colleague, or a manager at work; now do the same for someone who has affected your life in a positive way. Let yourself feel the difference as you shift back and forth recalling each person. The negative and positive feelings are rooted in the kind of relationship you've had with each, and give more of a sense of the significance of what we are talking about. I am guessing that if you try to be more specific about each relationship you'll be considering the presence (or not) of such qualities as trust, acceptance, respect, honesty, support and appreciation. Such qualities form the background and backdrop to all we are and do, shaping a sense of ourselves and our outlook on life.

In coach education and training, learning models and skills are often in the foreground as they give an important sense of what to do and how to do it. It is easy in this context to lose sight of the more relational aspects of practice (for example, at a very basic level, do I trust the other person?), or if relational aspects are addressed, to do so in terms of models, techniques and skills (for example, learning the theory of 'emotional intelligence' and the 'skill' of empathy). Such learning is important, but relational learning involves something additional that is in many ways more subtle and challenging; it involves active involvement in, and cycles of, reflection on relationships. I have found that this kind of learning is deeply and unavoidably *personal*, involving learning about myself and how I am in a relationship. It involves raising awareness of my thinking, feeling and behaviour and my part in co-creating relationships with others. Such learning can, at times, be somewhat painful and disturbing; by the same measure it can be very exciting and liberating. When the learning is painful and disturbing it is very easy to turn away from it, back to safer territory, and I often see this happen – where the whole process is dismissed as indulgence, as misplaced 'therapy'. However, my proposition is that such personal development work sets the bar for professional practice at the relational level, and in that sense personal and professional development are two sides of the same coin.

You can test out this proposition as you read the book, as throughout we'll see that relational practice is always rooted in personal involvement, an involvement which has more the character of a 'journey' than of a place where you've arrived with the journey complete. I know that, on a daily basis in my practice, I am constantly challenged in how I co-create relationships, a challenge I may meet more or less well. I also know that such work is the most deeply rewarding – it is the heart of what we do.

Take some time to reflect upon my proposition: that personal development work sets the bar for professional practice at the relational level. What are your thoughts about this?

- Does it make sense to you?
- Do you agree with me or disagree?
- How do you view the prospect of engaging in such personal development work?

SOME CONTEXT: THE 'RELATIONAL TURN' IN THEORY AND PRACTICE

I'd like to set the scene by briefly describing how the place and significance of relationship have been understood in counselling and psychotherapy (henceforth 'therapy'). I've chosen to do this because therapy is a discipline that has had to address the concept of 'relationship' throughout its long history, and in doing so has encountered the same kind of fundamental questions we shall have to address. In addition, as you probably already know, much of the theory and practice of coaching has its roots in therapy (Wildflower 2013; O'Connor and Lages 2007) and many of the various approaches to coaching are explicitly based upon therapeutic models (see, for example, Cox et al. 2014).

I have used the notion of 'relational turn' because, as we shall see, the story is about how relationship 'came in from the cold'; from a place of suspicion and 'repression' (i.e. as something potentially dangerous and pushed to the background behind theory and technique) to being the vital heart of therapy. In their early years both the psychodynamic and humanistic traditions sought to minimise the significance of the relationship between the client and the therapist. The concern was the same for each: to ensure that the therapist did not **influence** the client. Freud, in his desire for psychoanalysis to be seen as scientific, insisted that the analyst be a neutral presence, a blank screen, so as not to in any way influence the outcome of therapy. For the human potential movement (e.g. person–centred, gestalt, transactional analysis) born out of the social protests of the 1950s and 1960s, the issue was not about being 'scientific' but about freeing people from the damaging and constricting conformism imposed by culture – the internalisation of 'shoulds' and 'oughts' that stunted personal growth and prevented people actualising their innate potential. The task for the humanist practitioner was to ensure that the client found their own answer 'within', without being influenced in any way by the power and authority of the therapist.

This desire not to influence the client had a similar effect on both traditions: each tended to view the client as a separate self-contained being who had the 'answer within', with the therapist as another separate self-contained person who deployed models and techniques to enable the client to unlock their potential and find their own truth. The power of this view is evident today and fundamental to coaching. Indeed it has been said that 'In many ways business coaching is the human potential movement gone corporate' (O'Connor and Lages 2007, p. 28). So we are not dealing here with arcane historical curiosities but with cherished ideas that still excite and inspire, ideas that you may also hold dear. Coaches are still cautioned that the cardinal sin is influencing the client; that skills and models are the vehicle used to enable clients to find their own way uninfluenced by the coach.

The 'relational turn' (Mitchell 2000) refers to the way the significance of the relationship became apparent, both in theory and practice, in what might playfully be called the 'return of the repressed'. In the psychodynamic tradition, one of Freud's great insights, and the foundation stone for much subsequent therapeutic practice, was the concept of transference – a notion that arose out of his work with clients. He came to realise that his clients were relating to him as if he were a figure from their past, reliving their hopes, fears and conflicts in all their emotional intensity, in the here and now of the therapeutic relationship. With this realisation, 'relationship' became the centrepiece of therapy. From the 1950s analysts became increasingly interested in what was termed countertransference, understood as the impact on the therapist of the client's transference (perhaps evoking in the therapist feelings of anxiety, boredom or excitement), and the ways the therapist could use the countertransference as a basis for their interventions. The here-and-now experience of both participants in the encounter were involved – the therapist and the client. Like it or not, the therapeutic relationship became the site for revealing – and the crucible for hopefully addressing – the client's 'ills'.

At the same time as the relationship was becoming central in practice, so too it became the focus in the development of theory. In the UK, with object relations (Gomez 1997) and attachment theory (Bowlby 2005), and in the USA, interpersonal and relational approaches (Mitchell 1988), the significance of early relationships in the formation of personality became understood in ever greater detail, and the playing out of the needs, wishes and desires of both client and analyst in the therapeutic relationship became ever more evident. This new understanding was reinforced by developments in infant–parent research, aided by the use of slow-motion recording technology (Stern 1985; Beebe and Lachmann 2002), which demonstrated the exquisite moment-by-moment attunement of baby and parent, and how this attunement is built into the very fabric of the personality of the child and the way they come to relate to others.

With these developments in theory and practice it became evident that the notions of neutrality and 'blank screen' were hopelessly inadequate and misleading. It became clear that the client's issues were both made manifest in, and had to be addressed through, the relationship between client and therapist. One aspect of these developments is worthy of particular note. It became clear that successful therapy was not so much founded on skill and technique (though these are important) but on the quality of the person-to-person relationship – the sense of a real meeting of two people sharing a common humanity, and with it the tension between the personal and professional aspects of practice. Concepts had to be developed to make sense of the complex involvement of both parties in the relationship. Notions like intersubjectivity, co-creation, dialogue, mutuality and authenticity replaced neutrality and blank screen, generating some extraordinarily sophisticated, sensitive and moving accounts of the dynamics of the therapeutic relationship (DeYoung 2003).

A parallel shift towards relational theory and practice has taken place within the humanistic tradition. The same themes, issues and challenges have emerged. How should we understand and work with the reality that therapists cannot any longer view themselves as mere facilitators of the client's own process? That they are involved in the relationship? Rather than go into the history of this shift I'll give one example that I think nicely illustrates the developments and issues involved. Carl Rogers, the founder of the person-centred approach, in his first book *Client-Centred Therapy* (2003, first published in 1951) had in effect two 'core conditions' for therapy: unconditional positive regard (UPR) and empathy. UPR is a concept that demonstrates Rogers' commitment not to influence the client. He was aware that clients are always acutely sensitive to any hint of approval or disapproval; indeed they are looking for, expecting and wanting judgements as a guide to how to act. So in practice UPR means that the therapist consistently 'prizes' (values, appreciates) the client whilst making no judgements about the worth or merit of any particular aspect of what the client may think, feel or do. She wouldn't be saying things like 'well done' or 'that sounds like a good idea' as such words are likely be taken as indications of approval, which have the effect of influencing the client's behaviour. The second core condition, empathy, as you probably know, is putting yourself in the shoes of the other person in order to understand their experience in the world.

Rogers offered both UPR and empathy, which together paradoxically amounted to a humanistic version of neutrality and a blank screen, as the clients were only having their own experience played back to them. Rogers was challenged about the way he 'disappeared' himself from the relationship, and this led to the introduction of a third core condition: 'congruence'. Congruence is about 'being real' in the relationship. The tension between UPR and congruence is obvious and profound; how can I be equally accepting of everything when I may also find myself delighted, frustrated, bored, angry or excited by what the client is saying? Congruence is a thoroughly relational term. Increasingly, Rogers put more and more emphasis on the importance of being real, transparent and authentic, and towards the end of his life it became the most important of the core conditions (Lietaer 1993).

So in the psychodynamic and humanistic therapeutic approaches the significance of the relationship has taken centre stage. Like it or not, the practitioner is involved and will influence what happens. What has also become apparent is the understanding, born out of experience, that what is most 'healing' is the involvement in and experience of a relationship where the client is able to share what excites, shames, angers, frightens, matters and makes life worth living, with a practitioner who is concerned (and cares), trustworthy, skilled and who can genuinely bring themselves into the relationship without imposing their views (Cooper 2008). This is quite a challenge for both participants.

OUR RELATIONSHIP, AS WRITER AND READER

Writing about the significance of relationship invites the question: what kind of relationship shall we have, as I write and you read this book? I am struck with the parallels here with coaching, and with coach education and training. It is always a question for me about how to 'be' in these relationships, particularly the edge between the personal and professional.

What kind of relationship am I seeking with you and how will I go about putting that intention into practice? The choice is not free and unconstrained. As in all situations there are background conventions and expectations about the 'proper' way to behave which, rather like gravity, draw us into certain familiar patterns of relating that feel right and are likely to be accepted by the other person without question. The normal background convention in writing a book like this is to adopt a third-party form of address, such as 'This book is for people who ...' This feels unremarkable, safe and properly professional. Yet at the same time it invites a kind of distancing, the first moves in setting up a relationship where I as the expert adopt a 'tell' approach to you. I'm sure you'll see the irony here, given that this is a book about coaching. In this way, hardly noticing what has happened, the fundamentals of our relationship are put in place as we settle down and I tell you all about the coaching relationship.

So let's return again to the question: what kind of relationship do I want with you in the writing and reading of this book? I begin by assuming a shared interest and excitement about coaching, and a desire to explore it more deeply. From working with many people at different stages of development as coaches I have a sense of some of the issues, anxieties, excitement and confusion that you are likely to experience. I want you to do your own thinking about what I'm writing, and come to your own view as to whether you agree with me or not. So along the way I shall explicitly ask you to reflect upon the views expressed and how they tally with your thinking.

From my side I want to write in a way that resonates with how I am as a coach and educator, which in turn is based upon the kind of philosophy and approach you'll find in this book. I want to bring myself in and 'show up' in an honest, open way, sharing what I believe, where I get confused, and when I get anxious, excited and moved. I believe that the core challenge for us all as we get more deeply into relationship in practice is the tension between the personal and professional, and realise that the people who have had the most impact on me (and what I aspire to) embody both in a way that empowers others. It is a tension that is lived with and never resolved. In the face of anxiety the temptation is to shift into a defensive professional mode; on the other hand there is the anxiety of revealing too much, crossing a line, and being too personal. I fully anticipate that this tension will be present throughout the book, and if it isn't then something important will be missing.

To coin a phrase, there is no 'view from nowhere' (Nagel 1989), and there is also no 'voice from nowhere', so to begin to 'bring myself in and show up' I'd like to give you some of my background to enable you to place where I'm coming from as a context for what I shall be saying.

The existential question of the meaning and purpose of life has always haunted me and was the prompt for going to university, first on to a psychology degree and then, because the psychology was too biological and statistical for me, transferring to a social psychology and sociology course. This led to a PhD (Pelham 1982) which had as its focus the philosophy of science as interpreted and applied in the behavioural sciences, more specifically the behaviourism of B.F. Skinner, the staunchest advocate of psychology as a science.

After the PhD the fundamental questions of meaning and purpose were revitalised by a move into therapy. I worked in a psychiatric day centre and trained with Relate, which then was primarily psychodynamic in orientation, and at the same time trained in humanistic therapies. These two orientations came together when, for a number of years, I was the manager of a therapeutic community which gave me a sense of the power and importance of community and culture. From the psychodynamic tradition I have taken an appreciation of how our upbringing profoundly shapes our relation to self and others, and the many ways we protect ourselves from unacceptable thoughts and feelings, in ways that we are not aware of. The humanistic tradition offers similar understanding alongside a deep commitment to respecting the potential and autonomy of other people and their ability to make decisions about their own lives.

For many years I described myself as having a psychodynamic awareness alongside a humanistic way of relating. In the 1990s, seeking to find a way of integrating these differing views, I was drawn to the writings of American psychoanalysts who were developing what they called 'relational approaches' (Mitchell 1988), offering a very subtle and rich understanding of human relations. These relational approaches have since become widespread across therapeutic approaches (Pelham et al. 1996; Paul and Pelham 2000; Pelham 2008), and are a significant source of current interest in relationship coaching (de Haan 2008; de Haan and Sills 2012).

Around 2000 I began training in coaching, founded on gestalt, and this has again significantly shifted my thinking and practice, particularly in terms of the importance of contact and genuine meeting in the coaching relationship. The most profound shift over the past decade, however, has been towards an existential phenomenological approach, particularly as developed in the philosophy of Martin Heidegger (1962). This confronts directly the question of meaning and purpose, but also the importance of culture in forming who we are, and the challenge of 'taking a stand on our being' – i.e. taking ownership of our lives against the background of the expectations of the culture of which we are a part. I have found this perspective to be very powerful as a basis for coaching.

I take this background into workshops and programmes on coaching in the UK and Ireland, meeting a range of people – from those new to coaching, to people who have significant experience and are seeking to learn more. They also come from a variety of backgrounds – from CEOs, senior leaders and managers in very performance-driven multinationals, to leaders in the public and not-for-profit sectors, to people who are already independent coaches or consultants. Many of the programmes are also 'in-house', that is, delivered within organisations, often as an element of the development of a 'coaching culture' working with people in all levels of the organisation.

Who do I imagine I am in conversation with as I sit here and write? What comes strongly to mind is being in a workshop with a group of people, and the challenge of reaching out and meeting diverse points of view and differing needs. You may be at the beginning of your journey and be excited about the prospect of getting started, or perhaps you are somewhat sceptical of this whole 'coaching malarkey' and are biding your time so as to come to your own judgements about it. Overall I anticipate a keenness to get started and also probably some anxiety about it all, particularly the prospect of the practice, with both real coachees and the practice sessions that are likely to be part of your programme. The chapters of the book are written to address the development of you as a coach, with later chapters taking us deeper into the coaching relationship. So my view of you will change as I have a sense of talking to a group with more experience of coaching (and it may be that you pick up the book as someone already in a more experienced position).

I expect you are seeing some of the challenges and issues for coaching that arise from this understanding of the significance of the relationship. There is both clarity and comfort in the belief that there is an agreed theory, technique and skills which the coach simply has to apply to get the desired results. This clarity and comfort thins out when the significance of the relationship is understood, and concepts like co-creation, dialogue and genuineness take centre stage. The reality is that your hopes, desires and way of being with others will be in the mix, as will the coachees'. You are at least 50 per cent of whatever happens in the coaching, whether you choose to acknowledge it or not.

WHAT WE SHALL BE COVERING

The overall intention of this book is to act as a resource as you first become involved in learning about coaching and the coaching relationship, and as you develop your practice – initially with pro bono coachees, and then paid coaching with coachees in organisations. The final chapters consider wider professional issues on supervision, personal development and evidence-based practice.

Chapters 1 and 2, 'Getting Ready' and 'Getting Started', introduce the fundamentals of coaching as you prepare to meet coachees, and cover what needs to be in place in those first meetings. We'll draw upon the gestalt theory of perception, with the concepts of figure and ground, both as a context for awareness raising, which is at the heart of a coaching approach, and as an integrating theme throughout the book.

In Chapters 3 and 4 we'll focus on the 'psychological dimension' of coaching, and introduce a model of 'self and relationship management' which will be a reference point throughout the book. Using this model we'll look at key concepts such as anxiety, feeling and emotion, transference, countertransference, use of self and contracting, and the significance of these concepts for the coaching relationship.

Chapter 5 is entitled 'Widening the Field', where we'll use the gestalt notion of field to explore how the coaching relationship and coachees' agenda are embedded in, and arise from, a network of relationships, and then consider mood and emotion from this perspective.

Chapter 6, 'Culture, Difference and Diversity', deepens our exploration of the field, focusing on gender, class, sexuality, disability and so forth, which so often remain in the background, and are frequently the source of anxiety and confusion in the coaching relationship.

Chapter 7 addresses the transition from pro bono to paid coaching, as you conclude your initial coaching programme, take the 'L' plates off, and take on the identity of coach. The focus will be on your involvement with organisations (as an external or internal coach), and the chapter considers key issues such as who the client is (the coachee or the organisation) and the challenge of managing the complexity of overlapping relationships and dual roles.

In Chapter 8 we look at the place of supervision in coaching, and also address directly the requirement for, and challenge of, personal development, with the proposition that personal development sets the bar for the capability to work effectively with the relational aspects of coaching.

Chapter 9 explores the 'evidence base' supporting the focus on the coaching relationship, considering evidence primarily from counselling and psychotherapy. At the same time it attends to what might be termed the 'relational aspects of research', to provide a critical perspective on the research process and the notion of 'evidence-based practice'.

The Conclusion is entitled 'Putting Your Signature on It', with the message that although there are models, techniques and skills common to coaching, we all find our own way of doing it, co-creating with the coachee a particular and unique relationship. Finding your own authentic style is the ongoing challenge.

I want this book to be a practical resource for you, so throughout there will be references to working with coachees. To protect confidentiality none of the 'cases' are real coachees; rather they are formed thematically from work with coachees.

I think you will get the most out of this book if you take time to reflect upon what you've read, and take note of its impact on yourself. Such reflection is at the heart of developing as a coach, as you attend to the thoughts and feelings evoked in yourself, about how the reading connects with your own experience. It is likely that as part of your programme you keep a journal, and it could be useful to write your responses to my questions there.

KEY POINTS FOR PRACTICE

At the end of each chapter I shall identify some key points for practice for you to consider.

I've given you some of my background, knowing this has powerfully shaped how I am as a coach and educator. I'd like you to similarly consider:

- The route that has brought you into coaching and how your personal and professional history contributes to the kind of relationships you co-create with tutors and delegates on your coaching programme.
- The significance of this background to the kind of relationship you see as appropriate for coaching.
- How you'd characterise the kind of relationships you establish in everyday life.

RECOMMENDED READING

At the end of each chapter I'll also offer some recommended reading that can take you deeper into the content and themes we've been exploring. So in relation to this Introduction I suggest:

De Haan (2008) *Relational Coaching: Journeys Towards Mastering One-to-One Learning*. De Haan is the author who has brought the relational approach into coaching, and this book will be relevant throughout the subjects we cover in this book.

Gallwey (1986) *The Inner Game of Tennis*. Many see this book as marking the beginning of coaching. It is short and very readable. His concepts of Self 1 and Self 2 epitomise the humanistic approach, with Self 2 as the source of innate creative potential and Self 1 the constricting voice of cultural conformity.

O'Connor and Lages (2007) *How Coaching Works: The Essential Guide to the History and Practice of Effective Coaching*. This book provides a very readable and useful account of some of the origins of coaching which will supplement the account given in this Introduction.

Wildflower (2013) *The Hidden History of Coaching*. This book provides a detailed account of the psychological heritage that has profoundly shaped coaching.

My background in psychodynamic, humanistic and existential approaches, as described in this Introduction, is the source of much of what I shall be saying in the forthcoming chapters. There are other approaches that do not figure in my practice so clearly (for example, cognitive, behavioural, neuro-linguistic programming, solution focused) and I tend not to use psychometric/personality instruments (such as the Myers–Briggs Type Indicator, or MBTI), and therefore these perspectives and resources are not covered in this book. If you would like to know more about these approaches I recommend you supplement your reading with books such as Cox et al.'s (2014) *The Complete Handbook of Coaching*, and Palmer and Whybrow's (2007) *Handbook of Coaching Psychology: A Guide for Practitioners*.

1

Getting Ready: Gathering the Resources to Begin Coaching

I like the metaphor of a journey for describing the kind of experience you are likely to have as you get ready for coaching, because there is no doubt that you'll have a sense of having travelled some distance by the time you complete your programme and feel ready to say 'I am a coach'.

In fact the metaphor touches something very real, as delegates regularly say they are on a journey, and knowing them and the changes they have been through I can only agree, often in a very moving and heartfelt way. It is a journey of personal and professional development, and it is very likely that on your own journey you too will make some important decisions about your life and its future direction. Coaching has that effect.

So what resources do you need to get ready to meet your first coachee? Let's look at four, and consider the relational implications of each:

1. Clarity about what we mean by coaching.
2. A theoretical framework for practice.
3. The skills to implement an awareness-raising coaching approach.
4. A way of structuring the session.

1. CLARITY ABOUT WHAT WE MEAN BY COACHING

As we shall see, there are many definitions and descriptions of coaching, but it's important that you ask yourself this question first because it's likely you'll already have much of the answer. Coaching is a familiar word, used in a variety of contexts, and it's possible that you, or people you know, have already had some involvement with it.

Before reading on, jot down your understanding of coaching:

- What is it?
- What is it for?
- What are its core principles?

In doing this you will begin to establish your own viewpoint which will no doubt shift and change, but you will have begun to articulate your own position from which to evaluate what I and others are saying.

Here are some definitions – see how they line up with your understanding:

> Coaching is the facilitation of learning and development with the purpose of improving performance and enhancing effective action, goal achievement, personal satisfaction and fulfilment of potential. It invariably involves growth and change, whether that be in perspective, attitude or behaviour. (Bluckert 2006)

> Coaching is about change and transformation – about the human ability to grow, to alter maladaptive behaviours and to generate new, adaptive and successful actions. (Skiffington and Zeus 2000)

> Coaching is a process that enables learning and development to occur and thus performance to improve. (Parsloe 1999)

> Coaching is unlocking a person's potential to maximise their performance. (Whitmore 2009)

My view, which is rooted in the existential approach mentioned in the Introduction, draws on the metaphor of journey. It is about assisting someone to gain a sense of direction and purpose, which is often lost in the absorption with everyday life, and then set out on their self-chosen path. Coaching is about enabling someone to find their own next step, and to take this step in a skilful and effective way.

How do these definitions and my view line up with, differ from or shift your view of coaching?

However you position yourself amongst the overlapping definitions, the most fundamental principle of coaching is that ***people have the capability to take responsibility for, and make decisions about, their own lives, rather than someone else doing this for them***. This statement is highlighted as it is the bedrock for all that follows.

Like any manifesto, such a statement is easy to sign up to, and in my experience it strikes a deep chord in people. Yet it can be an extraordinarily hard creed to live up to because we live in a culture where people are told what to do, through advice, suggestions, direction and instruction. Telling is a deep-rooted habit. Parents, friends, teachers, doctors, you and I: most of us do it and do it most of the time. If you want the evidence for this just listen to others and to yourself. You'll hear variations on: 'What about ...'; 'I think it would be a good idea to ...'; 'Have you tried ...'

There are profound personal and professional issues in play here, as the tell approach is based upon what might be termed a 'deficit model' of relating, i.e. the person I am talking to lacks something which I will provide. Culturally this attitude is rooted in familiar background practices that are so taken for granted that we hardly notice them, and which create expectations on both sides: for example, going to the doctor for advice about what is wrong and what to do. At a more personal level, for most of us, for much of the time, there is a pervasive background belief that the other person lacks something or cannot manage, and therefore we have to step in and provide what is needed. This tendency is likely to be reinforced by a sense that my self-worth is at stake: to be of any value, of any use, I must be able to offer something to help, and this 'something' takes the form of telling. Telling is often driven by the anxiety of not knowing what else to do and the fear of being useless.

> I'd like you to take some time to think about what I've said here and consider whether it tallies with your own experience.
>
> - What part does 'tell' play for you as a parent, as a friend, or in your professional life?
> - What is your first move when someone is in difficulty?

What about from the other side of the coin? What is your experience of being told? Do you want advice and guidance? Do you invite it? How do you react? I know for me there are times when I do want to be told, for example when I go to the doctor. I also know that at times I have a visceral reaction against being told, and can get quite angry. It may be, for example, that I am about to go into an important meeting and someone starts to give me advice about how I should handle it; or I set off in the car and the person next to me tells me the route I should take.

If this sounds familiar, then the fundamental personal and professional challenge is developing the belief that people have the capability to make decisions about their own lives; they don't need me to do it for them. The expression from transactional analysis 'I'm OK – you're OK' (Harris 2012) catches the basic stance of coaching. It means that, in essence, we are both capable of taking responsibility for our lives. It alerts me to the possibility of two familiar shifts in the relationship: 'I'm OK – you're not OK', and 'I'm not OK – you're OK'. In the first situation (which leads to 'tell') I think I am more capable than you and that you need something from me. In the second situation I think you are more capable than me, and I want you to tell me what to do. The expression is a sensitive measure of whether or not I am in the right kind of relationship with you. I recommend you try it out for yourself.

What is involved in implementing the belief that other people have the capability to find their own way forward? We shall see below that there are a range of skills that you can learn that are fundamental to coaching, and are good to have in place when you meet your first coachee. But before we get into the details of those skills, let's consider more broadly what is involved in helping someone find their own way.

You'll recall from the Introduction that from a relational point of view the coaching relationship is co-created. Put simply, you as the coach will inevitably influence the coachee. How can this be compatible with the coachee's autonomy and responsibility? This is a hard question, and one to which we shall return repeatedly throughout the book as we explore more deeply the issues involved. Nevertheless, some initial thinking is important, if for no other reason than to avoid falling into the position of believing that coaching is mostly about models, techniques and skills, which if properly applied will be all that is required – a position that tends to treat people as objects, as passive 'things' to be changed ('If I do **this** – use this model or skill – then **that** will happen').

One way into this is to think about how you are in other relationships when you want to be of assistance, whether as a parent, a friend or a colleague. What is involved? Where is the line between enabling and taking over? The basic question remains the same: do you believe that the other person has the capability to take responsibility and make their own decision? If you don't believe in their capability then you're likely to tell. I know I am most prone to tell when anxious, so have to watch out when I notice anxiety stirring in me. A more useful response is to ask myself, and maybe the other person, what is needed and how can I meet that need in a way that respects their autonomy? For example, you might say something like 'Tell me a bit more about that' or 'What are your thoughts about it?' The notion of 'resourcing' can be useful here: how can you help resource the person, both internally and externally, to enable them to address what matters? And when is something other than asking appropriate – when perhaps they are so overwhelmed by a situation that something more is needed from you? These reflections are flagging up that whatever we choose to do will influence the relationship, and the choices made as to the best course of action are a matter of personal and professional judgement. In coaching, the same sort of judgements have to be made, and at times it is hard to know what is best to do.

There is real value in addressing these issues during coach education and training. There is a great opportunity to examine, in practice, your usual taken-for-granted habits of intervening, and get an understanding of the triggers that invite you to act in certain ways. In the initial stages you'll probably feel the strain of holding back from what you normally do, as you develop a mindset and the skills that offer you the choice of doing something different. It is likely you'll initially feel deskilled as you restrain from familiar behaviours and learn new ones. These skills will open up new possibilities in your relations with others, and widen the range of responding. They won't take away some of the dilemmas you'll encounter, but they will offer greater awareness and additional ways of resourcing others.

2. A THEORETICAL FRAMEWORK FOR PRACTICE

If we are to change our usual habitual ways of working it's important to have a framework that makes sense of, and provides guidelines for, this different approach. All that follows in this book is founded on the notion that 'meaning making' is fundamental to being human. We are always seeking and attributing meaning to events, from the smallest act of perception (e.g. that moment of confusion when a 'fly' nearby is suddenly a 'plane' a long way away) to the broadest social, political and philosophical systems. The 'facts' never 'speak for themselves', they only do so from within a pre-existing set of beliefs. This becomes obvious when, for instance, we hear politicians from different parties argue about the same issue, but differ completely and systematically about the nature and meaning of what is going on. In a sense they live in 'different worlds'. No doubt you've regularly experienced the same sort of thing when you've had disagreements with family, friends and colleagues at work – people see things very differently; the facts differ depending upon the viewpoint.

The gestalt school of psychology explored this meaning making in perception in the early decades of the twentieth century, and their analysis is important for us here. Gestalt is a difficult word to translate, but it basically means that the whole is more than the sum of its parts, and that, crucially, when we perceive something we do so immediately as a meaningful whole. For example, I hear a car door slam, or footsteps along the path, rather than a collection of different sounds which I then add together to infer what I've heard. The gestalt psychologists gave many examples of how we immediately ascribe meaning, 'completing' patterns that go beyond what is given to perception (see Figure 1.1).

I would anticipate that you will find it hard, if not impossible, not to see a panda, a circle and a rectangle in Figure 1.1, yet in fact each figure is incomplete. The 'panda' is an arrangement of black marks on a white background; the 'circle' and 'rectangle' are just some broken lines.

FIGURE 1.1 Completing incomplete patterns

The gestalt psychologists demonstrated that in an ambiguous situation there is the possibility of seeing more than one meaningful pattern, using what are now very familiar images (see Figures 1.2 and 1.3).

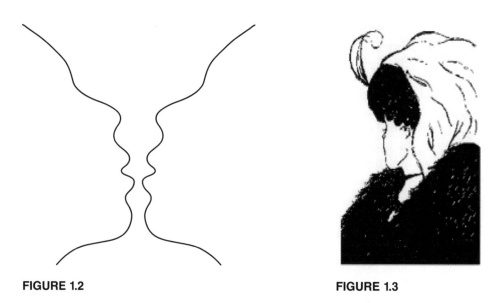

FIGURE 1.2   **FIGURE 1.3**

You can probably easily see the vase/faces and, perhaps less easily, faces of a young/older woman in Figures 1.2 and 1.3. Notice again that you'll be seeing each as a meaningful whole – for example, either as a black vase or white faces (rather than black marks on white backgrounds).

Notice in addition that you'll not be able to see both images at the same time, e.g. you'll not be able to see both young and older women's faces in the same moment (though you may switch perception from one to the other very quickly). This is because perception is organised around meaningful wholes, which the gestalt psychologists analysed in terms of 'figure' and 'ground', concepts that will be important throughout this book. The 'figure' is the something we 'see', the meaning we attribute to what we perceive: so the figure may be the black vase or the white faces, or the young or older woman's face. Each figure takes on meaning through a particular way of organising the 'ground' (short for 'background') – the 'source material' for the figure. For example, the black and white patches that form the mouth and chin of the older woman become the neck and choker of the younger woman. In a sense, the 'ground' becomes invisible, integrated as it is into the figure.

What is the importance of all of this for coaching? First, the coachee's issues, goals and agendas arise from the meaning they are attributing to the situation – their 'interpretation' of events. In other words, certain ways of making sense of situations have become 'figural' ('My manager always takes the other person's side against me'). All that happens, all the self-evident 'facts', are interpreted in terms of that figure – even events that might seem to challenge the dominant figure ('Yes, he seemed to take my side then, but he was only doing so because you were there; he didn't really mean it').

Second, this dominant figure (with its fixed meaning) shapes and limits the possibilities of action – possibilities that only reproduce the existing situation ('Well I suppose I could just ignore it' or 'Well I think I'm going to challenge him on it next time it happens'). For something new to happen, a 'fixed gestalt' (i.e. fixed way of interpreting the situation) has to be loosened to allow the possibility for a new figure, a new understanding, to emerge (like the switch from the face of the older woman to the face of the younger woman).

How do we loosen the grip of the existing figure? The approach taken throughout this book is that we do so through the process of raising awareness; we constantly invite the coachee to attend closely to their experience of the situation, the figure and the ground, and through so doing anticipate that new figures will emerge – new ways of making sense of the situation. If and when a new figure emerges it often happens as a sudden moment of realisation, an 'a-ha' moment, when the whole situation is seen anew (suddenly seeing the different face). This new understanding changes the terrain and opens up additional possibilities for action ('OK, I can see that I always feel that people takes sides against me. I need to work on this').

Let's turn now to how we go about this; how, in concrete terms, do we raise awareness?

3. THE SKILLS TO IMPLEMENT AN AWARENESS-RAISING COACHING APPROACH

Let me describe a scenario that is commonplace in the first coaching practice sessions and which you too may experience. Your coachee begins by outlining their situation and their difficulties, and having got to the end of the story there will come a moment when the coachee sits back and it is your turn to speak. At this moment there is often a palpable sense of the responsibility for 'solving' the difficulties shifting from the coachee to the coach, and it is likely that you will experience a sense of the responsibility landing with you, along with a keen sense of anxiety regarding what to say next. In this situation, even though you are primed not to and are hardly noticing what you are doing, you are likely to find yourself drawn into giving advice, or, mindful that you are not supposed to do so, feel at a loss as to what to do next. The question is: how do you go about implementing the coaching ethos and translate coaching principles into skilful practice?

There is a useful mantra that catches the spirit of what to do next: ***ask not tell***. The coachee has the answers. Your job is to ask questions, or use other skills, to help them find those answers. And it is important to underline that these skills are carriers of the relationship; they play a vital part in building the relationship.

You will experience for yourself – as observer, coachee and coach – the powerful relational impact of these skills when used well or poorly.

Good attention and deep listening. Participants on workshops who witness an experienced coach working with a coachee are often astonished by how little the coach actually says and how closely they attend to and listen to their coachee. There is often shared agreement from those watching that they would normally have 'jumped in' much quicker and would have been unable to tolerate the long silences.

The coach and coachee typically have a different story to tell. Usually neither is aware of anything special about the silences; rather the coachee often speaks of a deep sense of connection with the coach, of really being 'heard', and in that hearing they listen more to their own experience, becoming more aware of what they think and feel, and of how they behave. The coach is likely to have a similar experience, of connecting to the coachee and getting a deeper understanding of their situation, often becoming very moved by it and finding that what they need to say next and when to say it come forth without effort, without having to think beforehand 'What is the next thing I should say?'

Developing the capacity to really listen, and the confidence that what needs to be said will just emerge (rather than having to plan what to say), come with experience, and it is likely that developing this capability will be a challenge to you that takes effort and some self-discipline at first. It involves putting aside all the other things that tug at your attention and instead tuning into the coachee and what they are saying. One of the great pay-offs for you as a coach, something that participants on programmes discover to their delight and relief, is that when listening deeply they find that what to say next is 'called out' without having to anxiously prepare beforehand what to say.

Conversation is turn taking, and after you have listened it will be to your turn to speak. What can you say that does not involve you taking responsibility for the subsequent direction of the conversation? How can you avoid 'taking the reins', and instead enable the coachee to deepen their awareness of their situation? Paraphrasing, summarising and empathy are powerful skills that are fundamental here.

Paraphrasing is listening to the coachee and then passing the meaning of what they have said back to them. You may use the coachee's own words, or it may be that you use words that are similar but not the same, as long as they closely catch the same meaning. For example:

Coachee: I'm feeling a bit overwhelmed at the moment. We are being just a bit too successful, as many of the bids we have recently put in have been accepted but we haven't got enough resources to manage it all. And it is all landing in my lap to sort out! There isn't the time, and clients are increasingly unhappy because they don't think we are giving proper service – and I know we aren't. I just feel constantly stressed and cannot switch off even out of work time.

Think of how you might respond here. Maybe write down what you might say. You could take the reins and say something like:

> Well, have you thought of prioritising?

Or:

> Don't you think it would be a good idea to speak to your manager, as it is clear that something needs to happen to deal with the workload?

Or:

> It's important to separate work from home; you need to find a way to switch off, to properly look after yourself.

Or you could take the paraphrasing option, saying something like:

> So the business is doing well and there is lots of work coming in, but you're the person having to manage it all, and it's too much. You know the clients are right to be dissatisfied. All this is leaving you constantly stressed and worried, unable to switch off, even at home.

On paper, such paraphrasing can look artificial and stilted, and on being first introduced to paraphrasing people often laugh and say something like 'They'll just say I'm repeating what they've just said'. However, in practice – and when done in a skilled way – this does not happen, and paraphrasing is experienced seamlessly as a natural moment in an ongoing conversation.

What, then, is the value of paraphrasing, and why do we do it?

- It ensures that you accurately understand what the coachee has said. If you have not understood, the coachee has the opportunity to correct you.
- It demonstrates to the coachee that you are carefully attending to what is being said – this may be a new and powerful experience for them.
- It ensures you follow rather than lead the coachee. This allows the coachee to unfold their story at their own pace and in their own direction. It allows you to take your turn without taking responsibility for the direction of the conversation.
- It assists the coachee in gaining a little distance and objectivity about their situation. Your paraphrasing allows the coachee to 'hear' what they have said, and this helps in gaining clarity about the issues. In a way, with your paraphrasing, the issue is moved from a perhaps inarticulate 'something' within the coachee to something more definite that sits in the space between you, something you can both have a perspective on. It brings more to the fore – makes more 'figural' – what is normally just the 'ground', and in doing so allows the possibility of new meanings to emerge.

- It allows you breathing space, particularly at the beginning of the session – a moment to gather your wits and tune into the coachee. This can be very helpful, particularly if the coachee is conveying a complex story, the situation seems very stuck, or you feel under pressure to respond with an 'answer'. Paraphrasing gives you something to 'do', something to say, so that you take your turn in the conversation, begin to get the story out, and not grab the reins.

A very practical question may come up when you first try this out – when to paraphrase? It is likely to be most appropriate when you first meet a coachee, when all the information about the person is new, and/or when the coachee tells you a lot of (sometimes fairly complex) information and you need to ensure you understand. You'll also experience that moment when if you hear much more information – then you'll begin to forget the 'story', like a container about to overflow, and this is often a moment to intervene.

When you first try out paraphrasing you may be unsure about how to do so without seeming impolite or intruding, especially if the coachee is in full flow and speaking without leaving convenient pauses. The important thing is to indicate your wish to understand them, saying something like 'Can I just stop you for a moment so I can check I've got what you are saying?' or 'So what I hear you saying is ...' Usually coachees don't feel intruded upon, and instead hear your words as part of the normal turn taking in conversation; they listen to what you say and respond accordingly.

The real magic of paraphrasing is that after you have spoken, the coachee most often picks up from where you've left off and says more about their situation, often going in a direction that is surprising, even surprising themselves, as a new theme or thread emerges – 'figures' which would be lost if you'd stepped in and asked a question about an aspect of the story that seemed important to you.

Summarising is similar to paraphrasing. It reflects back the content of what the coachee has said but over a more extended period of time, and so is likely to be used later on in the session. Like paraphrasing it ensures the accuracy of understanding, but it also does something extra, which is important. It is a way of gathering up the themes, strands and elements of the whole story, putting them alongside each other, and in doing so helps the coachee clarify confusions, contradictions and conflicts, and perhaps find coherence and direction in what they are saying. You can also summarise when the coachee seems stuck, has apparently reached a dead-end, or when the session has lost focus and seems aimless. Summarising at these times can be likened to throwing all the pieces of the conversation into the air, and often the coachee will listen, perhaps sit back a bit, and then take one aspect of the summary as the next natural step to follow.

Empathy is perhaps the most basic, most fundamental form of human contact there is. Extensive research has shown that for both infants and adults the capacity for, and experience of, empathy is at the heart of well-being and good relationships throughout life (Goleman 1999; 2007). To be understood by another person is one of the most deeply meaningful experiences we can have. Empathy is often described as standing in the shoes of the other person and seeing the world through their eyes: the 'ground' of their being. This is a good metaphor because empathy is rooted in our shared humanity and shared culture, so that as I put myself in someone's shoes I can grasp what the world looks and feels like from that position, and it is from this basis that I can reach out to the other person and have a relatively well-founded sense of their experience in the world. Empathy is often referred to as a skill, but skill is only the external form of a fundamental capacity and intention to tune into another person in such a way as to catch, in all its complexity and feelingfulness, the other person's experience.

Have there been occasions when someone has listened deeply to you and you've felt understood by them?

- What was that experience like for you?
- What difference did it make to your understanding and involvement in the situation?
- What was the impact on the relationship between you and the person you were with?

Though fundamental to human experience, there are many blocks and barriers to empathy and it will be a vital aspect of your personal development, in service of your professional development as a coach, to address them. These blocks and barriers include fixed assumptions and prejudices about people, an unexamined certainty about what is happening (perhaps because you've 'been there' so feel sure you already understand, or based on preconceived theoretical assumptions), a reluctance to enter into the emotional experience of the other person, and a lack of awareness and experience about taking an 'empathic stance', i.e. the movement to trying to grasp what the other person is experiencing in all its fullness and immediacy.

Empathy can be categorised alongside paraphrasing and summarising as one of a group of 'reflecting skills'; indeed paraphrasing and summarising can be viewed as stepping stones to empathy. On first meeting someone you'll have little or no understanding of their situation, and paraphrasing and summarising can be used to build a picture of their circumstances. Then there is a gradual movement from this outside, external stance to entering more into their world, stepping into their shoes, and in so doing gaining a sense of what it's like to be confronted by their situation, with its conflicts, uncertainties and possibilities. It's likely you'll feel emotionally moved as you tune into the other person, and it is most likely that the relationship between you will deepen.

This careful listening to another person and actively striving to see the world through their eyes is the first step in empathy viewed as a skill. The second, vital step is communicating this understanding to the other person. It is not enough for you simply to have an empathic understanding; to be interpersonally significant you must communicate that understanding to the other person. Most often, but not always, this communication is through the use of words. Empathic understanding ***does not seek to change anything***, rather it is a human form of contact that says '***Yes I am with you, and I really want to understand what it's like to be you at this moment***.' Paradoxically, the experience of being understood is often a powerful stimulus for change.

For example, imagine a colleague comes to you and is very upset. He went to a meeting with his line manager hoping to get some support and advice about a difficult situation that he's very worried about. They had agreed a time to meet but she was 20 minutes late. She was clearly in a bad mood and rushed. They went into her office and he began to tell her about the situation, when her mobile phone rang and she then spent five minutes on the call. When the conversation resumed she listened only briefly before expressing frustration that he was bothering her with the problem and that she expected he would be able to sort it out, implying, he thought, that he was not up to the job.

As above, think of how you might respond here. Maybe write down what you would say. You could respond to this in many ways. You could say:

Well you know what she is like, she never gives anyone time or support.

Or:

Yeah, same thing happened to me with her last week.

Or:

Don't let her get to you; she is just having a bad day. I think she is under a lot of pressure.

Or:

I think Jo had a similar situation to deal with lately; try talking to her.

Or:

Never mind. Let me get you a drink.

Or:

Yes I can see you are in a difficult situation. Have you thought of trying ... ?

Responses such as these are familiar because it is sometimes hard to know what to do if someone is upset, and we usually wish to be of help in some way.

At the same time each of these responses would deflect, in one way or another, what my colleague is experiencing right now. How might you go about formulating an empathic response? Here would be my process:

Step one: active listening

The empathic response would form as I put myself in the other person's shoes and imagine what it is like approaching this particular manager with a problem, and notice in myself some anxiety at the prospect. I get a sense of this anxiety rising as the manager is late, probably mixed with irritation at being kept waiting. I put myself in their shoes as the conversation begins and the phone goes, waiting with anxiety and frustration whilst the line manager takes the call. Then I catch what it would be like to be spoken to in such a dismissive way

Step two: communicating my empathic understanding

As I seek to respond I try to catch what is at the heart of what my colleague is experiencing right now – the powerful mixed feelings about being treated that way, with the continuing unresolved situation still in the background. I say something like (and each person will catch and express this in their own way):

> So you've tried to get some help and feel you've been treated with no respect. I can see you're really upset and angry with her, and you haven't got what you need to deal with the problem.

The likely response to an empathic intervention is that (even though apparently hardly noticing it) the person feels 'heard', understood and now in a position to open up more on the situation, begin to reflect upon it and find their own way forward. For example, they might say:

> I *am* angry; how dare she treat me that way! But I'm still stuck. Maybe I need to sort things out with her first; try to clear the air.

Listening, paraphrasing, summarising and empathy are all skills that enable you to play your part in the conversation without taking control of it, and it's important at a practical level to have something to do, something to say, as an alternative to the 'tell' interventions. But it is clear that these skills do something more than simply give you something to do; you'll experience a deepening of the relationship, and often themes emerge in the conversation that come as a surprise to you both.

There is likely to be a sense of developing trust and also a certain tension in the air at the possibilities of what else might be said. So what is happening such that the coachees are beginning to understand themselves and their situation better?

This takes us to the heart of how raising awareness helps the coachee find their own way forward. Coachees know far more than they are normally consciously aware of about the circumstances in which they find themselves. In our everyday dealings in life we operate on the basis of tacit knowledge of situations that enables us to engage effectively without having to think about everything first. Tacit here means 'we can know more than we can tell' (Polanyi 2009). Coaching is about raising into awareness what we know but cannot yet tell. Through awareness raising we enable coachees to reconnect with aspects of the 'ground' that they know but cannot yet tell, and in doing so we enable new understanding to emerge. So raising awareness is at the heart of coaching; it is what coaches are constantly seeking to achieve through the interventions they make. It is an alternative route to 'tell'.

Awareness-raising questions and 'invitations to explore further': paraphrasing, summarising and empathy all involve playing back to the coachee what they have said. Questions and invitations to explore further are other powerful ways of raising awareness, and as such are central to coaching practice. They are used to invite the coachee to hold their attention on, and attend more closely to, their experience of whatever they are talking about. I liken this to looking at the sky at night. A quick glance at the sky may reveal a few stars. Take more time and attend more closely and many more stars emerge; they were already present but not yet in awareness. Likewise, I tacitly know far more about situations than I'm initially consciously aware of: awareness-raising questions and invitations to explore further bring into view (make explicit) what is present in the 'ground' but not yet 'figural'.

Here are some of the questions I regularly use:

- 'What is happening to you right now as you say that to me?'
- 'What are you aware of right now?'
- 'What else comes to you as you sit with that thought?'

Here are some invitations to explore further:

- 'Say some more [*or* tell me some more] about what happened between you and your manager.'
- 'Stay with that thought', or 'Stay with that feeling', or 'Let's just stay with that a bit longer.'

These questions and invitations hold the coachee's attention on what they are talking about, and what is happening for them as they talk about it. This process of raising awareness can be taken a step further by bringing the issue more 'experientially near', that is, more 'in the room', in the here and now of the session, so that the coachee can experience it more directly and deeply.

You might say, for example:

- 'As you said that your energy changed, you seem much more animated.'
- 'The expression on your face changed as you said that – what happened for you then?'
- 'You're telling me about your relationship with that direct report: what impact would it have if he were to walk through the door right now?'
- 'Imagine she is sitting here, on this chair, right now, what do you want to say to her?'

These are just a few of the kind of awareness-raising questions and invitations you can use. It is useful to have some examples of such interventions and try them out for yourself. Of course, there is a danger in taking these examples as things you 'should' say: a list to be learned. The important point is not to hold on to the particular words but the intention behind them – raising awareness. You'll see and hear many different ways of doing this, and find out along the way those that sit right with the way you work. Having said that, I have seen many people on training courses writing down the kind of interventions they have heard others use, or seen in coaching demonstration sessions, and said later how useful these formulations had been, and you might like to do the same. It seems that doing this provides a useful resource at the beginning; something for your own distinctive practice to coalesce around.

Your development as a coach will take place as you become more familiar with the kinds of skills described above. They are skills and therefore do develop with practice, ideally to the point where they become taken-for-granted, familiar, background ways of relating. They will change you and your relationships with others. I strongly recommend that you try out the skills in non-coaching situations, such as with family and friends, and at work. They can be used in a small way, such as one-off paraphrasing. Some of the most moving moments on courses have been when people have reported how paying attention and listening more, briefly reflecting back, or empathy has profoundly shifted relations between partners, or between parents and children. I vividly recall a person saying how his son got into a fight and the police had been involved. Instead of shouting at him, which was normal practice, he simply asked 'what happened' and listened. Everyone in the room was moved by his account at how this 'simple' beginning transformed what then happened in the relationship with his son. Trying out the skills in this way builds confidence and competence which you can take into your coaching with coachees.

4. A WAY OF STRUCTURING THE SESSION

Alongside the question of what skills to use is the question of how to structure the session. Structure is important in giving a sense of purpose and direction to the conversation: a sense that, to some degree, you know where you are going. The GROW model is the best known and most-used model in coaching, and has proved its worth as a way of structuring the conversation. I'll not go into detail as the model is described in many publications (Whitmore 2009), but I do recommend you read it and get to know it well. I'd rather offer a few thoughts about how you might apply it.

The four stages of GROW:

1. *Goal* – what do you want to get from the session?
2. *Reality* – what is the current situation?
3. *Options* – what are the possible courses of action?
4. *Way forward* (wrap-up) – what are you actually going to do?

The first stage is about establishing the goal for the session, which can be achieved by saying something as simple as 'What would you like to get from this session?' There are differing views about whether establishing a goal is helpful or not, as sometimes the coachee may not have a clear idea about what they want to talk about (Clutterbuck and Megginson 2013). They know there is something 'there' but do not have a sufficient grasp on what it is to be able to directly address it. In such a situation the 'goal' can be to talk about what 'it' might be, seeking to make explicit, make figural, the tacit sense of something that needs addressing, and this can be a very valuable thing to do and be clarifying in its own right.

However it is framed, whether as a goal or maybe a less focused exploration, inviting the coachee at the beginning to say what they want from the session is extremely useful in giving a sense of direction and purpose. It's something to navigate by in the subsequent conversation. It's likely that at some stage in any coaching session you'll feel a bit lost as to where the conversation has got to, or is going. Rather than you taking responsibility at this point to move the conversation along, you can use the agreement made at the beginning of the session as a reference point and ask the coachee about where they've got to and where they want to go next. It is also quite possible that along the way more clarity will be achieved about the subject under discussion, or that the initial goal will be superseded by other concerns, and it may be appropriate to renegotiate the contract at that point about the purpose and direction of the session. However it goes, inviting the coachee to identify what the session is about, and holding to whatever is agreed, keep the 'centre of gravity' of responsibility and initiative for the session with the coachee, a fundamental aspect of the 'ask not tell' approach.

'Reality' is the second stage, where the coachee is invited to explore their situation more deeply. The coach helps the coachee raise their awareness of what is going on and who is involved, paying attention to both the external world and their own inner world of thinking and feeling. In ordinary conversation this second stage is often missed out completely, or addressed in a very cursory manner, often leaping from goal to options ('I'm having problems with getting agreement from my manager about what has been agreed and I think she keeps changing the goalposts' ... 'OK, so what do you think you can do about it?'). In my view most of the work in the session should normally take place in the 'reality' stage, because it is here that we help raise the coachee's awareness of **what they know but cannot tell** – bringing into focus, making explicit and articulating that tacit, background understanding they already have of the situation.

When the reality stage is done well the final two stages tend to be relatively straightforward, as the way forward is very likely to follow naturally from the new possibilities arising out of the awareness raising.

I know that people new to coaching find GROW useful, then tend to dismiss it later as they get more experienced, often on the grounds of being too restricting as their practice develops. Personally I like it, as it is simple and effective, probably because it mirrors the natural stages of the process by which people identify and take their next step. It's also a useful resource if I get a bit lost in a session, as I can ask myself (and perhaps the coachee) about what are we trying to do (the goal) and where we have got to in achieving it.

A word of caution: Models are useful but it is important for you to consider your relationship with them. I have heard of occasions when people coming out of a coaching session say they have been 'GROWed', by which they mean they have felt they've been on the end of a process where the model dominated the session at the expense of sensitivity to what they needed as coachees. So I recommend that you familiarise yourself with GROW and other models of coaching but then hold them 'lightly' – as useful supports that can be damaging if they come to dominate your practice at the expense of the coaching relationship.

CONCLUSION

One thing that may surprise you, and that it is good to be ready for, is the kind of relationship with coachees that can quickly develop, even in what might initially seem like the artificiality of observed coach practice sessions. If you have a good structure to the session, carefully attend and listen to coachees, and invite them to more deeply connect with their own experience; this often builds a closeness and intimacy which is not present in normal everyday life. People often report – with a mixture of awe, anxiety, concern and delight – that in the very first session coachees say things which they have never told anyone before.

On reflection this is not surprising, as they are being invited to talk about something that matters to them; they are being listened to, and have the opportunity to explore what is going on. Often coachees report a sense of feeling 'lighter' – of renewed hope, excitement, possibility and purpose at the end of a session. How you respond is vital here and cannot be separated from how you are as a person. Can you allow this sense of closeness and intimacy, or does it raise anxiety in you (maybe named as concern about 'dependency') such that you pull back and become more 'business-like'? In my experience it is the people who can stay emotionally engaged, and see this as a 'normal' aspect of the coaching relationship, who become the kind of coaches who can be transformational for their coachees.

KEY POINTS FOR PRACTICE

The subjects we have covered in this chapter present some of the toughest challenges to people as they get ready to begin coaching, and you are likely to be similarly challenged. As preparation for practice:

- Without making any judgements about yourself, listen out for your own style in terms of asking and telling.
- Experiment with holding back from giving advice, suggestions and direction, and see what this is like.
- Informally try out the skills described in this chapter, maybe with family, friends or colleagues, as alternatives to tell: listening, paraphrasing, summarising, empathy, awareness-raising questions and invitations to explore further. You can do this in a small way – just 'one liners' – and see what happens.

RECOMMENDED READING

Shainberg (1983) 'Teaching therapists how to be with their coachees', in J. Westwood (ed.), *Awakening the Heart*. Though written for therapists, this is a delightful and very moving exploration of what it means to listen and pay attention, and the transformation that can happen. I strongly recommend it to you.

Rogers (2012) *Coaching Skills: A Handbook* is a book to buy as a resource, as it covers the core skills and other aspects as you start off and develop as a coach.

Whitmore (2009) is the classic text to read here. Many see it as having founded coaching in the UK. It is short and easy to read, giving a fuller description of GROW plus the importance of awareness and responsibility.

Clutterbuck and Megginson (2013) *Beyond Goals: Effective Strategies for Coaching and Mentoring* invites deeper consideration of the place of goals in coaching. If you wish to read some evidence-based studies around goals there is Grant (2012) 'An integrated model of goal-focused coaching: an evidence-based framework for teaching and practice', *International Coaching Psychology Review*; and Grant (2014) 'Autonomy support, relationship satisfaction and goal focus in the coach–coachee relationship: which best predicts coaching success?', *Coaching: An International Journal of Theory, Research and Practice*.

Clarkson with Cavicchia (2013) provides a good introduction to gestalt, written from a counselling perspective.

2

Getting Started: The First Session

CONTRACTING

By 'getting started' I mean taking what you are learning on the programme, and through your reading, and putting it into practice with coachees. This is a major step, and it is good to spend some time thinking about what is involved. The programme provides the setting with the necessary conditions for a coaching conversation to take place; that is, in coach practice sessions the coachee (because they are colleagues on the course) has a sense of what coaching is about ('ask not tell') and a safe, secure, confidential environment for them to explore in depth whatever they wish to talk about. If these conditions are not in place then coaching won't take place, and to the extent these conditions are eroded, the coaching will be eroded. The task you have when you meet pro bono coachees is to put in place the same conditions, and this may be a challenging thing to do because, for example, it is likely that she or he has little or no understanding of what coaching is about, and may be wanting all sorts of different things from you. Likewise, finding a safe and secure setting may not be easy.

Setting up these conditions usually comes under the heading of 'contracting', and, when supervising coaches, I find that many of the difficulties they bring have their roots in the contract, and addressing these involves establishing the required contract. The word 'contract' is serviceable as it indicates an agreement with the coachee about what we will be doing: shared expectations about our roles and the setting. The downside is that it implies a very formal approach to what we are about, carrying an implicit focus on a written contract that specifies the conditions of the meeting. Delegates on courses often become very focused on this formal aspect, on what should go into that written contract, and are keen to see examples. Tutors can at this point look rather uncomfortable, because there is likely to be a wide range of practice. Some coaches may have detailed written contracts, others more minimal statements, perhaps in an email, of the agreement that has come from the first meeting (depending on how the conversation went).

How can it be, then, that proper contracting is fundamental to the success of coaching, but creating a detailed written contract is not the main issue? The answer is that we are referring to a wider process than the written contract; we are referring to the fundamental process of setting up the coaching relationship – agreeing how we are going to work together and the conditions under which this can happen. Contracting 'frames' the relationship, and like a picture frame it sets up a space that is different from everyday life. It sets the boundaries of the coaching relationship, demarcating a separate and distinct protected arena where a different kind of conversation can take place. If a picture frame is 'wrong' (e.g. the wrong size, shape or colour), or it is broken in some way, then this immediately affects what is within it. Likewise with the coaching frame, if it is not properly in place then the coaching will be out of shape or the boundary between coaching and everyday life will not be clear.

Establishing the coaching frame in practice may not be easy. Many people you meet who agree to coaching will have little understanding of what coaching is, and be even less clear about the conditions required for it to take place properly. Your task will be to set up the coaching relationship, and once it is set up, hold it in place. There are issues of power and authority lurking here, understood in terms of 'good authority' (Pitt-Aikens and Thomas Ellis 1990). Good authority is the positive use of power for the well-being of those in a particular relationship. It is noticeable often by its absence, when things fall apart. For example, good authority is putting in place appropriate boundaries and then holding to them. This is the basis for trust, a trust that can easily be lost if agreed boundaries (for example, of confidentiality) are not kept. As the coach you are invested with the authority of your role: it is you who understands what coaching is and the conditions needed for it to happen; it is your responsibility to communicate this and ensure that they are established in practice. In doing this you may find that coaching is not what the coachee wants, or they may not want to do it in a setting that is suitable. Good authority is holding to the conditions that make coaching possible and being prepared to forgo the opportunity to work with the coachee if the proper conditions cannot be agreed.

I hope you can see now that there is more at stake in contracting than a written agreement. Such a document can be useful in mapping out some of the territory, establishing in a formal way some of the boundaries, but the 'contract' is established and its meaning becomes clear only in practice. It is through the ongoing relationship which you co-create that you work with the tensions, possibilities and limitations of an 'ask not tell' approach, and live through the pressures, inconveniences and necessity of holding to proper boundaries.

Take a few minutes to consider for yourself this process of contracting:

- What do you think are the fundamental conditions that need to be in place for coaching to be viable?
- Will you have a written contract, and if your answer is yes, what will you have in it?

Contracting as you begin coaching can be particularly challenging. You are likely to be quite anxious at the prospect, wondering how it will go – 'Will I be any good at it?' Then there is probably a pressure, driven by the requirements of the programme, to get coachees; and you may get to a place where (as time runs short), to put it bluntly, 'anyone will do'. There is a third factor in play that is less obvious but pervasive, which arises from the fact that most coaching during training is offered pro bono. There is a strong tendency for this to create a sense that coachees are 'doing you a favour' and therefore you must accommodate to their wishes and needs, particularly around when and where you meet. Sometimes a certain mood may creep in that the coaching, because it is free, is not being taken seriously and that it is acceptable for sessions to be cancelled or rescheduled, sometimes at the last minute. These three factors – the anxiety, the pressure to get coachees and the belief that the coachee is doing you a favour – may combine to make it hard to hold on to the good authority required to get the relationship right as you start coaching. Paradoxically, it may be when you first start coaching on a pro bono basis that a written contract is most useful, as a way of signalling to the coachee and also to yourself that the work is to be taken seriously; it's a professional relationship, not a favour.

Let's take an example of 'getting started', which is illustrative of the issues we've been looking at and entirely typical of what may transpire. Imagine you are in a group supervision session, perhaps on your coaching course. What do you think are the issues to address, and what do you think should happen next?

Mary is in a senior position in an IT department of a large finance organisation. She lets it be known to friends and colleagues at work that she is on a coaching programme and was looking for people to coach. A colleague at work has a friend called Jane in another organisation who 'could do with some help', to whom he had mentioned the possibility of coaching, and this person expressed interest in taking up the offer. Mary contacts Jane, first by email and then by phone, and they agreed to meet. It turned out that Jane was on sick leave and wanted to meet at her house. Mary was a bit uncertain about this, but could not think of another place to meet, so agreed. They sat down to talk in Jane's kitchen and Jane made them both a cup of tea. Mary could hear there were other people in the house, one of whom briefly came in to say hello.

There were a couple more interruptions – a postal delivery and a brief phone call, which Jane answered. Jane works in the housing department of a local authority and was off work due to stress brought on, she said, by the sheer volume of work created by the cuts in staffing levels over the past few years. She felt overwhelmed, with no one to turn to, as her colleagues are similarly overworked. She also spoke of a number of very difficult family circumstances, including her elderly mother who lived some distance away, on her own, who needed 24-hour support, but refused the option of moving into a care home. Overall she seemed depressed and somewhat hopeless. There had been a session on Mary's course about contracting, around confidentiality, agreeing a goal, the number of sessions and so forth, but she came away from this coaching session feeling somewhat confused, concerned and uneasy with the whole set-up.

> What are your thoughts about Mary's first session and how she felt on leaving the session? Make some notes in light of the discussion above on contracting and the coaching frame. Consider the following:
>
> - Is there is a proper frame in place for coaching?
> - Is it coaching that is required?

I'll share my thoughts as if I too was listening in a supervision group, and see how they line up with what you've written. As indicated earlier, when supervising coaches I always listen out first for the contracting as this is the source of most difficulties, which are typically experienced by the coach as a sense of unease, anxiety and confusion. There are two headlines for me: the agreed setting and what the coachee wants/needs.

First, does the setting provide the secure confidential space that is required to establish the kind of relationship needed to explore issues in any depth? There is a kind of informality about meeting in Jane's home: a tacit, unstated blurring of the boundaries between personal and professional which erodes that confidential space. This lack of appropriate boundaries becomes more apparent as the friend pops in to say hello and Jane answers her phone. If this situation continues I'd be confident in saying that the coaching will never really get started, though they may spend many sessions together.

Second, there is no clear sense of what the agenda is, as Jane has spoken about her work and personal life without settling on anything specific. This may be fine, as sometimes it takes a while to get clear, and doing so can be important in itself. But in this case there is a more pervasive sense that the personal and work lives are entangled, and her mood raises questions of what is most needed: is it coaching or perhaps counselling? I'd flag up my sense of the lack of a clear agenda, and the uncertainty as to whether coaching is what is needed.

> Drawing upon your own thinking and my thoughts above:
>
> - What might you say to Mary about the setting?
> - What would you think if the coachee was a man who Mary was seeing in his home?
> - Is it coaching that would be best for Jane rather than, say, counselling?

I hope you are beginning to see the fundamental importance of contracting in setting up the coaching relationship, and can reflect upon the implications of this example for your own practice.

I'd like to share some concluding thoughts on this example before we move on to consider another, as I've often heard of pro bono coaching taking place in peoples' homes. Do you think it is ever acceptable to coach someone in their home, and, if so, what needs to be in place for a proper coaching relationship to be established? As I see it, the main issue, after considerations of safety, is the lack of control you have over what happens, and I have heard many situations, ranging from the bizarre, to the worrying, to the funny, of situations that have arisen. In a similar vein, do you think it is OK to coach someone in your home? Again, it is quite common practice, particularly with pro bono coaching. What are the benefits, and what might you have to take care about?

Let's consider a second example to see what issues are raised and what might need to happen to put in place a secure coaching relationship.

John is head of HR in a large retail organisation based in a town in the north of England. He too let it be known to friends and colleagues that he wanted to get some coachees. A colleague in HR in another similar organisation in the region said he could put John in contact with Andrew, who is a really bright young talent and would benefit from coaching. Andrew was keen and they agreed to meet in a hotel lobby with plenty of quiet spots where they were unlikely to be disturbed.

Andrew is in his mid-thirties, developing a career in sales. He loves his work but he was feeling angry and frustrated with his manager and the organisation. He came over as restless and agitated, saying he felt he was being unfairly treated and passed over for promotion. He was considering taking out a formal complaint as he could see others whom he considered to be of less experience being promoted before him. He was pleased to meet John and felt sure that, with his HR background, he could help him with the complaint. John made it clear that as a coach he was not going to advise Andrew what to do, but that he'd be pleased to help him think it through for himself. Andrew seemed a bit deflated by this response but wanted to meet again to talk more.

They agreed a date, but Andrew cancelled the session at the last moment, saying he had to be at an important event. The second meeting took place with John trying to help Andrew explore what was going on at work and his relations with his manager. Andrew seemed to be stuck in a sense of injustice and resentment and tried a number of times to get John's views on how he was being treated by the organisation and what he might do to get redress. He seemed frustrated with John's refusal to give advice. John left that meeting feeling uneasy, knowing he would not be surprised if the next meeting was cancelled by Andrew.

As with the first example, imagine you are hearing this account in group supervision:

- What are your thoughts about John's sessions with Andrew and how John felt as he left the second session?
- Do you think there is a secure frame in place for coaching?

If I were listening to this in supervision I'd be wondering about a couple of things. The first concerns the setting and the suitability of coaching in a hotel lobby, which is very common practice in pro bono coaching. What do you think are the advantages and disadvantages of using a lobby? It is likely to be a mutually convenient venue and not cost anything to meet there. There will be some privacy, but at the same time that privacy is limited and this is likely to affect the quality and possibilities of the conversation. It will be particularly difficult for the coachee to explore strong feelings, so the conversation is likely to have a somewhat constrained and muted tenor.

A second issue is whether it is coaching that the coachee wants, or does he really want some form of advice? The professional background and expertise of the coach may be important here. It may be that you are of interest to your coachee precisely because of your background, and that they hope you will offer an informal kind of mentoring or give advice. Remember, most people don't know what coaching is, and it is understandable that coachees will initially expect to get from you what they get from most people, i.e. advice, guidance and direction. Though you may be as clear as you can be, and hold to the coaching approach, you may still be working at cross purposes, perhaps leaving you both somewhat dissatisfied and confused. In this case, the dissatisfaction is not clearly articulated by Andrew, but perhaps expressed in the cancelled session, and experienced by John in his sense of unease and uncertainty about the next session.

The examples of Mary and John give you, I hope, a sense of the issues involved in setting up your first coaching sessions. The ideal is a safe, confidential space and a shared understanding of coaching that meets the needs of the coachee. Meeting these conditions takes work and may not always be possible, but the coaching relationship will be eroded to the extent that the set-up is not right. Your motivation and confidence as a coach will be a significant element here: will you use 'good authority' to get the frame right? It is worth making this a priority as it will profoundly affect your coaching.

STRUCTURING THE FIRST SESSION

Managing the first session with a coachee can be quite challenging as there are a number of things that need to happen to properly set up the coaching. These include:

1. Starting to build the relationship by getting to know each other.
2. Explaining about coaching so there are shared expectations.
3. Getting into the story.
4. Contracting.

There are various ways of covering these points. It may be that you tell the coachee early on what you want to cover, or you just simply structure the session to ensure it happens. You may find that you do it differently with different coachees, as some may come in and launch straight into their story, whilst others may want to talk more about coaching and what's involved. However each particular session evolves, it's good to know the various strands to be addressed by the end of that first session.

1. Starting to build the relationship by getting to know each other

You will already have had some contact with the coachee when setting up the first meeting. However, it is important at the start of the first meeting to spend some time saying hello and talking together to find out a bit more about each other. It's up to you what to share about yourself, and you might want to give some thought beforehand about this. My attitude at the beginning is to 'get interested' in the coachee and see what flows from this in the conversation. Regarding how long you should take over this, again you'll find your own style, but there is a balance between getting to know each other and 'getting down to business', as the coachee will be wanting to get something from the session and it is important to create a sense of purpose and direction.

2. Explaining about coaching so there are shared expectations

As has been indicated in the examples above, it is quite likely that the coachee does not have a clear idea about coaching and will therefore seek from you what is normal elsewhere: advice, guidance and so on. Therefore there is a job to do in 'educating' the coachee as to what to expect and the kind of conversation you'll be having. This can be done in an informal way, perhaps by asking the coachee about what they know about coaching, and/or saying briefly that you don't have the answers but will help them find their own. What you say will set the scene and serve as a reference point, but may not initially carry a lot of weight; it is likely that the coachee will still anticipate that the conversation will follow the same old rules. What you say will only carry weight when you put it into practice, and then you'll find out how ready the coachee is to have a coaching conversation or whether they are really committed to something else. In the example above, Andrew was seeking to tap into John's experience in HR to provide guidance for his complaint, so a coaching approach was mostly frustrating. The first session sets the scene and gives you data as to whether coaching is what is wanted, and offers the opportunity as you conclude the conversation to talk openly about whether coaching is the right approach.

3. Getting into the story

This is where you will draw most clearly on the skills and the structuring (GROW) discussed in Chapter 1. The conversation will probably move on from the opening 'getting to know each other' to asking what the coachee wants from coaching. They may be very clear and specific about this, or it may need more time to surface and be given shape to. It may be that by the end of the session there is still more to do to identify a specific agenda, and this will have to be picked up in the next session. There is also a sense that, in an informal way, you will be doing an 'assessment' of whether coaching is appropriate. Peter Bluckert (2006) has a section on the 'coachability of the coachee' which I'd recommend you read, as the coachee may, for a variety of reasons, be either more or less coachable than expected. In the example above, Mary left the session with a concern about whether it was coaching Jane needed or something else, perhaps counselling.

4. Contracting

The coachee's story can be really engaging, and it is quite likely that the coachee will be very involved in telling it. It may feel hard, therefore, to draw that to a close so as to leave time to properly contract about the work. You will both have a shared sense of how the conversation went and whether coaching is likely to be fruitful, so you can explicitly ask whether this approach is what the coachee wants. You can agree on the agenda even if at this stage you recognise that settling on the agenda is still a work in progress. You will also address things like confidentiality, where and when sessions should take place, how long they should be and how many should be arranged, and whether and how you might have contact between sessions (e.g. email, text, phone calls). If there are course requirements that might involve the coachee (such as case studies or recording sessions) this would be a good time to talk about them and seek permission.

You can see that structuring the first session is complex; there is a lot to do. It will require you to exercise your authority as the coach and manage the session, allocating time for each aspect in a way that flows and respects the pace and rhythm of the session.

ACKNOWLEDGING THE PRESENCE OF EMOTION

When you create a situation that is safe and use the skills of awareness raising to help the coachee talk about something that matters to them, you'll find they often start to tell you things that are very private, things they have never spoken to anyone else about and perhaps have never openly acknowledged to themselves either. You'll start to hear the way they view the world and the kind of assumptions they make about themselves and others, their hopes, fears and ambitions. It is likely they'll come to speak about this in a very 'feelingful' way, i.e. with a lot of emotion. In the examples above, with Jane there were feelings of anxiety about her job, and she was upset about her mother and had a background mood of hopelessness and depression. With Andrew there was frustration and anger with his manager, and initial hope then frustration with John. Think how you'd respond to these emotions. Would you acknowledge them? Would you invite exploration of them? One thing is certain: how you respond is going to affect significantly the development of the coaching relationship.

Let me describe what I often see happening in coach practice sessions. Imagine that we're observing the conversation between Mary and Jane in such a session. Encouraged by Mary's attention and skills Jane begins to talk more deeply about her situation. As she talks her distress about the situation at work becomes apparent – in her tone of voice, her face, her posture and so forth. As she moves to talk about her family situation and her mother, the upset becomes even more apparent, with some tears forming. The mood in the room changes as the emotions become more present, predominantly a sense of rising tension and perhaps uncomfortableness. Initially Mary does not seem to notice the emotion, perhaps continuing to ask questions in a very matter-of-fact way about the situation. Jane seems to be embarrassed about the show of emotion and acts to 'pull herself together' and return to explaining the situation in a way that matches Mary's matter-of-fact tone. When the emotion becomes stronger and the tears begin to flow they cannot be ignored. Clearly uncomfortable, Mary hunts round for a tissue whilst reassuring Jane that it is perfectly under-standable that she feels as she does; anyone would do so in her situation. Having mopped up the tears they quickly move the conversation on to what Jane might do to sort things out.

In the debrief of the session Mary is asked about her experience, particularly around Jane's emotion. It becomes clear that she had hardly noticed Jane's emotion at first and that she'd been taken aback by the tears and didn't know what to do, but thought it best to get the conversation back to the situation at hand as she didn't think Jane would want to talk more about what was upsetting her. Jane is asked about her experience and says that actually it would have been good to go into her feelings some more. Mary is surprised by Jane's response but also somewhat con-cerned and agitated. There is a sense that there is something dangerous about 'going there', a bit like opening Pandora's box – what might get released? After all, this is coaching, not therapy; where is the line? It is almost as if acknowledging feelings takes us into therapy.

Put yourself in Mary's position:

- What would it be like for you to be listening to Jane when she became tearful?
- How would you respond in that situation?
- What do you think is the impact on the coaching relationship of addressing, or not addressing, the emotion that is present?

These can be tricky questions, and you'll have to come to your own view about them. My belief is that the coach's ability to empathise with, tune into and respond to a coachee's emotions sets the bar for the depth of the ensuing coaching relationship. At the same time, we live in a culture that is uncomfortable around emotions, one that distrusts them and is somewhat afraid of them, and therefore emotion is mostly ignored or 'managed'. It is this culture that can set the tone for how the coach is likely to respond to the coachee in the early stages of coaching.

How is it possible to become more open to the coachee's feelings and work with them effectively? This is as much a personal as a professional development issue. How comfortable you are around emotion sets the tone for what then happens. If you demonstrate in your manner that you are open to whatever the coachee brings – their excitement, anxiety, anger, fear, shame, happiness and so forth – then the coachee will take the message that it is OK to feel like this, and be ready to share more, explore more, delve into territory they are likely to be very uncertain about. On the other hand, if you are uncomfortable and anxious, then the coachee will pick up a sense that the feelings are not OK, and shift back on to safer territory, probably thinking and practicalities.

So how you are around emotion is the most important thing, and this is likely to challenge you in a fundamental way. If you are ready to engage more with the emotional aspect then the 'how to do it' is relatively straightforward, as you'll be using the same awareness-raising skills we've already discussed: listening deeply, empathy, tuning into and expressing the emotion that is present. Simply inviting the coachee to 'say some more about' or saying 'let's stay with that' raises awareness, as will drawing attention to what you see and hear in their manner: 'I notice your voice changed then'; 'your mood shifted as you said that'; 'that has brought the tears'. So with Jane you might say something like 'Let's stay with that anxiety, say some more about it', or simply, 'Speaking about your mother has brought the tears.'

Emotion is present in most coaching sessions and with most coachees, no matter what their position or seniority in an organisation, though it will be accessible to a greater or lesser extent depending on the context. Of course, there is a wide range of emotion and it can be just as important to recognise the presence of hope, optimism, delight and excitement as it is to recognise anger, fear and sadness. How relevant it is to attend to it is always a matter of judgement, as sometimes it will be present in a very background way, and addressing the agenda may require something different, perhaps clearer thinking. If you are uncertain as to whether to focus on emotion that is present you don't have to guess; you can ask (i.e. contract): 'I can see you are upset about this. Would you like to talk about it a bit more?' And if there is agreement to talk about it you can check in along the way that it is still OK: 'I can see you're surprised about how deeply you feel about this. Are you okay to stay with it?'

COACHING AND THERAPY

It may be at this point that you are beginning to share some of Mary's concerns: is going into feelings like this crossing the line between coaching and therapy? Where is that line? The skill set is very similar, so the difference will not be made obvious by auditing the skills that are used. The difference is in the intention. Coaching is always future oriented – about where we are trying to get to, our next steps and our involvement with the world around us in getting there. The coachee's internal world – in this instance her emotions – is relevant insofar as it enables or restricts the person in achieving those ends. Therapy on the other hand is more concerned with the internal world of the person. The intention is to enable the coachee to become more aware of their internal world and possibly change aspects that are troubling in some way or another. The internal world is always the reference point in therapy. When I am coaching someone I will invite the coachee to address their thoughts and feelings to a depth and extent that is relevant to the outcomes they wish to achieve from the coaching, and no further. Crossing the line would be exploring the coachee's internal world further than is necessary to achieve their coaching goal.

How do I know if it is really therapy rather than coaching that the coachee needs, and whether I should refer the person on? For example, with Jane there is a sense of depression and hopelessness, so should Mary continue or should she refer Jane to a therapist? This can be a genuine concern and the answer is not always obvious. The discussion above on the difference between coaching and therapy provides a basis for the answer. The coachee may have personal difficulties that are creating significant problems, which have a large part to play in the issues brought to coaching. In such a case, is there a definite, definable coaching goal and can we work towards that goal in a coaching way? If the answers to these questions are 'yes' then coaching is appropriate. If the answers are 'no' then coaching is not appropriate.

Often of course, the answers are not so clear-cut. In our example, the agenda is not yet clear and there is a sense of depression: does Jane have or not have the resources to make use of coaching? This is a difficult judgement to make and it would be important to take this to supervision (of which more later) to talk through what is involved, and if the judgement is made that therapy is the preferred option the question becomes how best to talk to Jane about this. There is a third option: could Jane begin therapy whilst also continuing with the coaching? Some people (especially those with a therapy background) might say no. I think it is possible, and know of a number of instances when it has worked well, where clarity about the coaching agenda has been established and the coachee perhaps invited to consider how therapy can contribute to the success of the coaching.

There is a lot to consider, then, as you get started in the first session. There is getting the contract right so that you are coaching in a safe, secure environment that gives the coaching the best chance of being successful. There is structuring the session so that all the necessary elements are addressed and the coaching has a sense of purpose and direction. And then there is developing the coaching relationship: getting interested in the coachee, tuning in to them emotionally, and using your skills to enable them to start telling their story.

KEY POINTS FOR PRACTICE

This chapter is about your first sessions with coachees, and you can use it to prepare and review. Consider how you are approaching these first sessions:

- Do you have a sense of 'good authority' to put in place the proper boundaries?
    - Is the setting safe?
    - Is it a confidential space that will allow you to talk about sensitive issues?
    - Is it coaching that is most appropriate, and is the coachee clear about what is on offer?
    - Reviewing the first session, is there anything you still need to address to get the 'frame' right?
- Are you clear about how to structure the different elements of the first session, and in reviewing it what is there to learn and take into future first meetings?
- Overall, how did that first session go?
    - How would you describe the kind of relationship you've established with the coachee?
    - What skills did you use and what have you learned from using them?
    - Were you able to structure the session, drawing upon a model such as GROW?
    - Were you able to engage with the emotional aspect of the session?

RECOMMENDED READING

Sills (2012) 'The coaching contract: a mutual commitment', in E. de Haan and C. Sills, *Coaching Relationships: The Relational Coaching Fieldbook*, is a thoughtful chapter that goes a bit deeper into contracting and explores the differing levels of contracts that are aspects of the coaching relationship.

Hay (2007) *Reflective Practice and Supervision for Coaches* is a good book, with a chapter on contracting and boundaries that includes contracting in organisational settings.

Gray (1994) *An Introduction to the Therapeutic Frame* is a fascinating text. It is written from within the psychodynamic therapeutic tradition and is not an introductory text for coaching, but it explores many of the more unconscious relational dynamics around 'the frame'.

3

Self-Management

What is it like sitting with a coachee once the initial getting-to-know-each-other and contracting are over? I want to share a sense of what this is like, but it is difficult to express. At one level the answer is simple (in concept if not in practice): I'm here to help the coachee succeed in reaching their goal and to do this through awareness raising, in ways we've already discussed. But at the same time it's not simple because I'm hearing a rich and complex story, and it can be hard to know which aspects to focus on as there are so many possibilities. Then there is the question of how the coachee and I are getting on together. What is the chemistry like between us, and how does this chemistry play in to what we are both here to achieve? From your first experience of being with coachees you'll probably understand what I'm getting at. What do I respond to amongst all I am hearing? What do I say?

There's a lot going on, and with it a growing intimation that how the coachee is as a person is at the heart of the whole thing. Are they excited or disinterested, emotional or very rational, taking responsibility or blaming others? We are not just dealing with a situation but a relationship with the person who is at the centre of it all. This may seem like an obvious point but the implications are profound. We're moving into what might loosely be termed 'the psychological dimension' (Bluckert 2006), or to use Gallwey's expression, the 'inner game' of coaching (1986; 2007). At times this prospect is variously exciting, daunting or humbling, and often the way forward is not clear. So how to proceed? Is there a roadmap which can give some orientation?

Marshall Goldsmith's (2012) 'What got you here won't get you there' is a great expression which provides some of the roadmap. It catches a profound 'existential' paradox which is at the heart of coaching. On the one hand, your usual way of going about things is 'what got you here'. This includes your everyday taken-for-granted ways of thinking, feeling and behaving, the kind of relationships you establish with others and, importantly, your particular strengths. It may be, for example, that you are successful because of your technical expertise in a specialist area, say IT or accounts. On the other hand, these strengths won't necessarily 'get you there' if, for example, you take on a leadership role which is fundamentally about influencing and developing others. In fact, your strengths may well lead you astray, as leadership is a different kind of task and your existing expertise is not what is most needed in the situation. You'll see that it is probably not just a matter of adding new behaviour to an existing set, because the change goes deeper than that, and is likely to challenge something fundamental about your usual 'way of being' in the world. You may need to challenge your 'ingrained patterns of behaviour' (Ridler & Co 2013).

When sitting with a coachee I hear about 'what got you here' – the coachee's participation in the events so far. I'm also likely to hear something about how this 'won't get you there' and realise that part of the task is going to be helping the coachee see how they are contributing to the situations they bring and the changes they'll need to make in themselves to 'get you there'.

I recommend you try out Goldsmith's expression for yourself:

- What is it about you that has 'got you here'? What are your strengths? Your commitment to hard work; your interest in people; your particular talents and interests?
- And how is it that what 'got you here' won't 'get you there'? What are the things you want to do that are hindered by those same strengths?
- What kind of work do you imagine you'll need to do to get from here to there?

SELF- AND RELATIONSHIP MANAGEMENT

I'm going to introduce two new concepts – self- and relationship management – which will deepen our understanding of why what got you here won't get you there. They are also concepts that we will repeatedly come back to through the book. They are drawn from infant research where slow-motion recording of infant–parent interaction has shown something of great importance. They show that in any relationship the baby is doing two things at the same time: they are managing the relationship with the other person whilst also managing their own self. In the world of infant research this has been called self-regulation and relationship regulation (Beebe and Lachmann 2002). I have adapted their diagram in Figure 3.1, using the word 'management' rather than 'regulation'. For our purposes they are roughly equivalent, and I think 'management' has a less mechanical, more proactive feel to it. These two concepts are at the root of developmental processes that shape personality and relationships.

Let me give an example of what I mean. A father loves playing with his daughter Helen, who is about six months old. He likes a game of 'chase and dodge' which

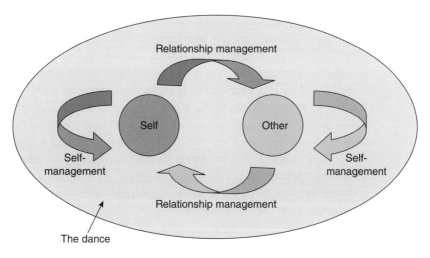

FIGURE 3.1 Self- and relationship management

Adapted from Beebe and Lachmann (2002)

involves getting and holding eye contact, 'getting in her face', laughing and smiling. Initially Helen likes this and reciprocates. Dad ups the game and chases her eye contact past the point that is fun for Helen, to a point where it becomes intrusive. She begins to show distress, signalling that the game isn't fun anymore and manages the contact with Dad's eyes by turning her face away so the contact is less. This behaviour only fuels the game for Dad and he persists, playing the game over and over again, chasing her eyes as she averts them, determined to 'win' the game. If you were watching this happen you'd probably feel a knot in your stomach as you'd feel the distress caused by this intrusive behaviour. Not able to evade Dad's eyes, Helen eventually gives up trying but does something else instead to moderate the contact. She goes limp and seems to withdraw into herself; her eyes glaze over and she stares into the middle distance. A pattern of relating is being formed that continues in other arenas, with Dad overinvolved, not reading the signals, and Helen managing her own behaviour, becoming more passive, apparently compliant, as a way of managing Dad's behaviour.

Self- and relationship management are two sides of the same coin. In switching off, Helen is finding a way of managing the relationship with her father, who is very important to her. She is apparently going along with what he wants, accommodating his dominating manner, but does so in a way that is tolerable to her. At the same time she is managing her own self, containing within herself the emotions that are bound to be evoked by such behaviour – of distress, anger and frustration – and behaving in a way that protects her from the intrusion. The gestalt approach has an appropriate term for this process: 'creative adjustment'. Creative adjustment indicates that each of us finds ways of adjusting our behaviour to meet our own and others' needs, though in the process we may compromise on something important to us.

Self- and relationship management provide a good model of how patterns of relating develop early in life and become the template for later relationships, a model backed up by extensive research (Beebe and Lachmann 2002). And it is precisely the patterns that 'got you here' which at the same time 'won't get you there'. It may be, for example, that Helen will become adept at tuning into and adjusting to the needs of others. What began as a creative adjustment has become a 'fixed gestalt', an ingrained pattern of interpreting and behaving. This capability is a strength that becomes very important in situations and roles later in life. At the same time it's unlikely she'll be able to get a clear grasp of what she needs and be able to assert herself to get those needs met.

As said above, self- and relationship management are two sides of the same coin. Nevertheless, there are different dynamics to consider with each, so the rest of this chapter will focus on self-management and we'll pick up the discussion of relationship management in the next chapter, though addressing one side always infers the other.

SELF-MANAGEMENT

I am sitting with a coachee, April, who is in the HR department of a large organisation. Her passion is working with people, wanting to help them develop. She is ambitious and wants to get to a position in the organisation where she can influence policy and decision making at a high level. She has just had a difficult meeting with her manager. She always feels criticised by him and has just had a poor appraisal. She is talking about this in a matter-of-fact way, saying how unfair it all is. As we talk more she becomes upset, on the verge of tears. Immediately she 'pulls herself together' and apologises. She feels quite ashamed at the show of emotion. In that moment, the surge of emotion was more alarming for her than the difficulties with her manager. She sees herself as someone who is strong and always does a good job, a bit of a perfectionist. She works hard trying to ensure everything is done right, though she knows there is always more to do and nothing is ever dealt with to the standards she'd like, so she always feels a bit vulnerable. The manager's criticisms strike a deep chord in her, though talking further it is apparent that the criticisms were rather minor and were set alongside a lot of positives. She wants to use the coaching to sort out her relationship with her manager, which she sees as endangering the development of her career.

We talk about what goes on between her and the manager. At first she says it's all his fault; he just doesn't like her and that's it. Besides, he is critical of everyone. No doubt he has his part to play in this but I'm also interested in April and her contribution. I invite her to tell me more about being hard working and a perfectionist and she says she's always been like that. She laughs and says when she got 90 per cent in exams her parents would say, 'What about that other 10 per cent?' I ask, 'What's it like being in a situation where you cannot be perfect?' She becomes more anxious and replies 'Dreadful!' 'So what do you do then?' 'Work harder and harder and he still isn't satisfied.' The self-control fractures and tears appear. After a few moments she gathers herself together and apologises profusely.

It's clear that April's usual self-management strategies of working hard and doing a perfect job are breaking down, overwhelmed by the pressures of the situation. It's a moment of threat and opportunity. The threat is of 'failure', not being successful. The opportunity arises out of these same circumstances, because something new is needed. 'What got her here won't get her there' (working hard, being a perfectionist) but it is a huge challenge to change such deep-seated beliefs, feelings and ingrained behaviours.

Is there more to say about self-management that will be useful here? Well you can probably see that self-management is fundamentally about self-protection. Self-management includes all the ways we have of managing ourselves in relationships that keep us safe in a way that enables us to get by and get some of what we want in the world. The particular forms of self-protection are mostly learned early in life and become deep rooted, shaping our personality. Freud's notion of 'defences', which is now part of our everyday language, equates with self-management. Freud (2003) said that defences are deployed to keep aspects of ourselves that are unacceptable out of our awareness. He listed and described many such defences, such as projection, introjection, repression, denial and splitting. I particularly like a similar expression used by Harry Stack Sullivan (Barton Evans 1996), who developed an interpersonal psychotherapy. He wrote about 'security operations' which people deploy to manage anxiety. His security operations had an interpersonal focus: children learn early the magic power of words; that if you say sorry, though you don't mean it, this is taken at face value or at least deemed acceptable, and gets you out of trouble; or 'as if' performances whereby a behavioural pretence (as if I'm pleased to see someone when I'm not) is deemed acceptable. There are many forms of self-protection which we'll not go into here, but I strongly recommend that you find out more about them (see, for example, Sandler 2011).

If I am going to help April to change then I'm going to have to help her explore how she defends and protects herself, as this is what locks her into the pattern of behaviour that isn't working for her. How are we going to do this? Somehow we have to find a way to loosen the grip of these security operations and allow the possibility of something new. I have my own formulation of the dynamics of self-regulation (which I think catches the essence of most psychological approaches) that may give a clue as to what is needed. It is a system involving three elements – anxiety, threat and self-protection (Figure 3.2).

Anxiety is what we are most aware of. For many, if not most of us, anxiety is a constant companion, just sitting in the background but then flaring up as something happens. Anxiety is a signal that somewhere there is a threat, which may be of something happening right now or something we anticipate happening. As anxiety rises so do the forms of self-protection. With April there is always a background of anxiety in the room which intensifies as tears appear.

Threat is the perception that something may happen or be happening that is bad or dangerous to us. This threat may be in the external world, such as poor

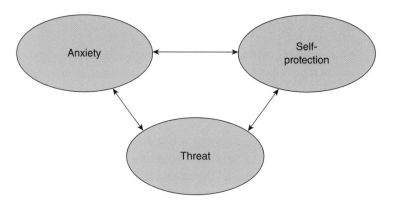

FIGURE 3.2   The system of self-regulation

exam results or a forthcoming presentation to a large audience. It can also be something internal to us; perhaps I'll think, feel or do something that will upset me (for April it was showing her tears). You can probably see that the internal and external are usually two sides of the same coin. I'm afraid that my presentation will go badly and I'll feel ashamed.

What is the nature of these threats? There are various sources but most, at heart, are threats in relationships. At their most primal level they are rooted in our needs around being loved, accepted, valued and included. These needs can only be met via other people so we are always at risk in relationships. Perhaps the most pervasive threat is judgement – being judged by others and judging ourselves, as it is through this that we discover whether we are acceptable, lovable and valued.

For April her sense of self-worth is rooted in being successful through hard work and doing a perfect job. The manager's criticism and the experience of being overwhelmed by the pressures of the job are potentially devastating. She fears being judged, found wanting and rejected by others. Behind the criticism of her manager is her own self-criticism, which is far harsher than anything the manager has said. The tears in the session were the most immediate threat. It was clear that for April there is something deeply shameful in showing emotion. She was harsh on herself and expected the same from me.

Self-protection is my term for the forms of self-regulation, self-management, defences and security operations that are deployed to manage the threat and lessen the anxiety. April's usual defence is also her strength – work hard, do a perfect job and maintain a tight grip on emotions. There was also sure to be a constant stream of 'self-talk' (Gallwey 2007; Stone 1993): an ever-present inner critic, just on the edge of awareness, which is another form of self-protection as it is monitoring her behaviour, keeping her in line and telling her that she is not working hard enough, and that she is being lazy and weak for showing emotion.

You'll see that anxiety, threat and self-protection together form a self-sustaining system. Anxiety whooshes up when threat is perceived and self-protection (defences) are deployed to manage the threat and the accompanying anxiety. This system protects but also limits; like an electric fence it protects a certain territory, is dangerous to go near and packs quite an (emotional) clout. At the same time it cuts us off from that 'dangerous territory', the other side of the fence; it makes it hard to learn from experience. We pull back and cannot test whether those same threats still apply and whether this habitual behaviour is still appropriate. Anxiety was ever-present for April, flaring up more and more as the threats to her mounted, culminating in the criticisms by her manager. The threats and anxiety drove her self-protection strategies, as she worked harder and harder trying to do an impossibly perfect job. The tears in the session were a real 'crack in the wall', which was even more distressing for her. But as you can see, none of her familiar ways of dealing with things were getting her any nearer to dealing with the challenges she faced – indeed, they are part of the problem.

I've introduced some fundamental and wide-ranging concepts here. To be able to use them it is important that you take some time to think them through, and to see whether they make sense to you and whether you can connect with them in your own life:

- Is anxiety a familiar companion to you?
- What are the situations where anxiety regularly flares up? What is the threat?
- Are you aware of ways in which you protect yourself in the presence of this anxiety and threat?
- Can you see the same kinds of processes in relation to other people, and particularly the coachees you have seen?

SELF-MANAGEMENT AND COACHING: LOOSENING THE TIES THAT BIND

The system of self-management is self-sustaining and a keystone of 'what got you here'. It can be understood in terms of figure and ground, where a particular figure (a particular way of understanding and behaving) has become fixed, locked in place by anxiety and forms of self-protection. How can you loosen the system's grip in order to create the possibility of 'getting there'? The good news is that the way forward does not involve learning new skills, but rather using and developing what we've discussed in previous chapters, with a deeper understanding of, and sensitivity to, the relational dynamics of self- and relationship management. Let's look at what's involved.

Managing anxiety

The coaching relationship is at the heart of it all. Self-management is driven by anxiety and is pivotal to shifting the system. Coaching is at its most effective and has the possibility of being transformative when there is an optimal level of anxiety present in the session and the coach has the sensitivity and skill to work on this edge, creating a situation that is safe enough for the coachee to go that bit deeper into the source of the anxiety and examine their usual ways of managing it. We are, in fact, seeking to loosen the grip of the system of self-regulation so that something new can happen.

What is an 'optimal' level of anxiety? If there is little or no anxiety present then it is unlikely we'll really get to the heart of what is going on. The coachee may well talk a lot and give a lot of detail – we'll be talking *about* what's going on, which may or may not be interesting, but at the end of the story there is likely to be a 'so what?' feeling; the talking is not likely to change anything. The coachee's self-management system is firmly in place; their anxiety is under control and the existing 'figure' unchallenged, so that nothing new is going to happen. There may be circumstances where the coachee is so well defended that if anything is going to happen it may be necessary to increase the level of anxiety in the room, perhaps by directly challenging some of the forms of defence, to use what Nevis (1997) calls provocative as well as evocative forms of intervention. I may point out that April constantly blames others for what has happened but doesn't seem to recognise she has any part in it, or that she changes the subject whenever I invite her to talk about something. For example, I may say something like: 'Your focus is very much on your manager, but I'm wondering about you and your contribution to what's happened.' Or again: 'I'm noticing that when I ask about your contribution you go back to talking about your manager.' Challenging in this way may seem somewhat 'rude' because it's not the sort of thing we normally say to each other, yet not to do so would, in a sense, be letting the coachee down. Such interventions raise the level of anxiety in the relationship and possibly open a route into more meaningful work.

On the other hand, the level of threat may seem so high and the anxiety so strong that the coachee metaphorically pulls back, withdraws or signals in some way their unwillingness to continue on this path as their defences go up even more firmly (maybe by changing the subject or insisting even more strongly that it is others who are to blame). The optimal level is where there is sufficient anxiety present to draw into view the nature of the threat and the coachee's normal way of self-protection, whilst at the same time feeling safe enough to explore it all. Fritz Perls, one of the founders of gestalt psychotherapy, had an apt phrase that catches what we are getting at: a 'safe emergency' (Clarkson and Mackewn 1993). This may seem a somewhat overdramatic expression, but it does catch something of the flavour of what it can feel like in that moment on the edge. The setting is safe *and* threatening. For April, the welling-up of emotion and the tears was a 'safe emergency'. The challenge for the coach is how to hold attention on that edge and how to help the coachee explore more deeply what it's all about – the nature of the threat and how they protect themselves. It is by this means that the ties are loosened and new possibilities emerge.

Building trust

How do I make the situation safe enough for the coachee to go that bit deeper? The most fundamental element is trust: there must be enough trust in the relationship to balance the threat. We've already discussed some key elements of trust. Contracting builds the safe space – the safe 'container' for the work and the manner in which I go about it – and holding agreements in place will set the bar for what can then happen. From this perspective we can again see why coaching in a hotel lounge sets serious limits on what can be achieved.

Judgement is perhaps the most fundamental issue. The coachee is always expecting judgement, and fears that they'll be found wanting, which is a primary driver for self-protection. Any hint of such judgements will close down the space for exploration and you can be sure that the coachee is listening out for them. This judgement can come in many forms, such as inferences that 'it's your fault', 'you're not up to it', 'you've acted badly' and so on. I have to confess that as I'm listening to coachees I sometimes have such thoughts, and it's likely that you do too. We can disguise these messages in different ways, but the coachee will soon pick them up. The difficulty here is compounded by the fact that I want the coachee to look at their part in what happened; so how can I do this without being critical, or coming over as critical? The heart of the issue here is that we are not neutral around people, and coaching is not a neutral activity: we all judge, it's part of the human condition.

There is a personal as well as professional dimension in this, and though the professional stance and capability is vital, at some deeper level it is the personal resonance that is most profound; does the coachee matter to me and do I show that? I find it hard to articulate clearly what I mean, but if I can connect with the coachee then something shifts in my manner and the relationship. A kind of intimacy and closeness builds, bringing with it care and concern for the coachee and a pleasure in the work we are doing together. Then my whole manner becomes appreciative of the other person, and judgements I make are set within this context.

I'm sure you'll immediately see the challenge here. It's not possible to have this care and concern when first meeting a coachee and it cannot be 'switched on' in a deliberate way; I'll 'click' with some coachees more than others. Yet I'm sure there is a direct relation between the quality of contact we have and the quality of the work we do together. In Chapter 4 we'll be looking at how some of the judgements we make are a vital source of understanding which can help us make more sense of the kind of relationships the coachee enters into. This does not absolve us, however, from the vital personal and professional work each of us needs to do to better understand the roots and impact of our own judgementalism, if for no other reason that they set the limits on the quality of the work we can do.

Listening for 'relational hot spots'

In all the complexity of the coachee's story there are certain things I am listening out for and will pay close attention to. I've called these 'relational hot spots' as they are the places where the anxiety is most strongly located, indicating there is something powerful at play here. I'm listening out for places of conflict, or more precisely, the places where the coachee feels most conflicted, as it is here that they are most stuck. These places are often signalled by a change in the coachee's manner: in their tone of voice or hesitant speech, or in their body language (perhaps turning slightly away or looking down). The emotional tone of the session is likely to shift, and though I may not know what it is about, my relational 'divining rod' (i.e. that intuitive sense that we've touched on something important) tells me there is something here to attend to. It's likely that I'm gaining a sense of what the issues are: maybe a conflict of loyalties, maybe a fear to do what's right, maybe a desire to take a course of action that will upset other people who are important. With April the obvious relational hot spot is with her manager, but I was also listening out for where she is most conflicted in herself. The tears signal there is something *right here* to attend to – there is something powerful going on about being strong and in control, and the shame when this is not the case.

The anxiety and emotion will surely be interwoven with some deep-seated assumptions the coachee has about what it means to be a good person – the kind of person who is valued and accepted by others – and I'm listening out for these. They are usually based on messages picked up in childhood and can often be heard in the language the coachee uses, particularly when they speak of what they 'should', 'must' or 'ought' to do. Such messages, as the coachee has translated them into their own lives, can be extremely powerful and the basis of their self-identity and self-esteem. It may be that 'duty' is fundamental, or 'not letting people down'. For April there was a sense that she should be perfect (not get 90 per cent but 100 per cent), hard working, and emotionally strong. But this strategy, though it got her to where she is now, is no longer working – in fact it is becoming damaging to her. The internal messages and the emotion are all bundled up and the coach can help by paying attention to and raising awareness just there, rather than all the other details of the story. If she can loosen the ties that bind her to past messages and emotion, then real change can occur.

Working with those relational hot spots

This chapter began by posing the question of what to do next once the 'opening moves' in the coaching have been completed. I'm going to gather up the strands of the discussion so far as a basis for answering that question. The basic proposition is that the patterns of relating we have learned, and that have 'got us to here', are often our strengths but also contain limits that hinder us 'getting to there'. These ingrained patterns of relating include the way we relate to ourselves, and to 'loosen the ties that bind' we have to become aware of those patterns, which is a challenging thing to do as they are emotionally charged and have deep roots in our sense of self-esteem and identity. This way of understanding things is in the background and provides an orientation for the coach who is listening out for, and attending to, 'relational hot spots' – those places in the conversation that are emotionally charged and have the greatest potential for transformational change. We'll now see how the very same skills we discussed in the opening chapters are relevant once more.

Good attention and listening. This remains fundamental, but now includes listening out for and attending to those relational hot spots. This new sensibility brings something else into the relationship. There is a readiness to create space that allows coachees to think and feel more deeply about themselves and to get more in touch with what is going on, because if you hurry them along by being too quick in your responses they'll feel harassed and lose some contact with what really matters (Kline 2009). As we sit in the shared silence there is often a palpable sense of an awareness forming, and the emotional tone of the session shifts as the coachee connects more deeply with their concerns.

Paraphrasing and summarising. With the new sensibility you may find yourself organising your interventions in terms of the conflicts you're hearing, particularly how the coachee is self-conflicted in the situation. You still seek to accurately gather up the strands of what you've heard, and the coachee will let you know if you've got it wrong, but you can pay particular attention to the relational hot spots. With April, I'm sure to juxtapose what she has said about her need to be perfect with the demands of the job which don't allow perfection.

Empathy. This is always at the heart of tuning into the coachee's relational hot spots. As you place yourself in the coachee's shoes you'll 'get the picture' and feel what it's like to be in their situation. Again, you'll be connecting with the conflicts that are present, especially how the coachee is self-conflicted. You may feel the sadness of leaving a job (where there are so many good friends) to take on a new post that offers exciting possibilities, or of having to say no to someone when this risks harmony and friendship. With April I can feel how important it is to do a perfect job and the anguish and shame that arise when this is not possible, and I can feel how distressing it is to show emotion when her self-image is about being strong and being able to cope.

Empathy also has another vital role here, as it is at the heart of building trust and creating a sense of safety. In building trust, nothing is more powerful than the experience of being understood. Empathy, by its very nature, draws one in and sets up a resonance with the coachee, such that we are likely to share laughter or tears. You'll notice we're at that risky edge between the personal and the professional, but it is just here that the deepest connection is made that opens the possibility of change. To put it in the more academic theoretical language used at the beginning of this chapter, it is precisely here that we can loosen the ties of the system of self and relationship management: empathy can create a deep sense of safety that allows for a heartfelt exploration of anxiety, fears and forms of self-protection.

Awareness-raising questions and invitations. As the coachee tells her story you can focus your intervention on the relational hot spots you're noticing. For example, you may be listening out for and paying attention to the coachee's deep-seated assumptions – I might say to April: 'Say some more about being perfect, about having to do every job perfectly', or 'What's it like for you when you've got too much to do to give proper time to everything?' I'll be paying attention to the level of anxiety in the room, and if she replies in a cognitive, uninvolved way I may seek to make the experience more emotionally present by bringing it all more 'experientially near' by saying something like: 'So, imagine you're at your desk right now surveying the work you have to do. What's that like?' The challenge for the coach is to use awareness-raising skills (including empathy) so that their work is on the edge between having enough anxiety to be engaging but not so much that the coachee closes down.

Acknowledging the presence of emotion. This chapter has been premised on the assumption that emotion is interwoven with the system and processes of self-management; the capability to acknowledge and work with emotion is not, therefore, just 'nice to have' but is fundamental to this way of working. It is the basis for recognising the relational hot spots and going with the coachee into those places. Quite a lot was said in Chapter 2 about working with emotion, and all of that applies here. As with the other interventions, there is now an added sensibility as to why emotion is so important. It is the key that locks in behaviour; at the same time, of course, it is also the key that unlocks behaviour.

Relational hot spots are always places of emotional conflict, and somewhere in the mix is something that matters to the coachee, something they want, something they desire. It is the feelings that accompany these desires that are the motors for coaching, that provide the impetus for coachees as they seek to loosen the ties that bind, and find a new way forward. With April it was the breakthrough of emotion that enabled us to get more deeply into both her fears and her ambitions. She wanted to reach a position in the organisation where she could make a difference, and it was this desire that fuelled her determination, her ambition and the possibility of overcoming the existing self-imposed limits. As a coach I need to empathise with and support this side of the emotional equation whilst fully acknowledging the vital role played by the current 'creative adjustment' in getting the coachee to where they are now in life.

Is this therapy? Chapter 2 concluded with a discussion of the line between coaching and therapy, and the views put forward in this chapter may mean it's useful to revisit that question as there is no doubt that the way of working described here involves exploration of the psychological dimension of coaching. The kind of practice advocated here is coaching and not therapy, and the line stays the same as described in Chapter 2. The line is set by intention. The intention in coaching is to help the coachee reach some future-oriented goals, to get from here to there. The coach helps the coachee explore their inner world – in the language of this chapter, their ways of self-management – as far as is needed to create the freedom to achieve those future goals, but no further. With April, we'll explore her inner world to raise awareness of how her self-beliefs are holding her back from progressing in the organisation, and to the extent that it helps her achieve her goals it will be sufficient.

IMPLICATIONS FOR PRACTICE

In this chapter we've looked at the 'self-management' aspect of self- and relationship management:

- Can you apply the notion that 'what got you here won't get you there' – that their strengths may at the same time be limiting – to your coachees?
- What is your reaction to the focus on the 'psychological dimension' in this chapter?
    - Does the 'system of self-regulation' make sense to you?
    - Do you think you can work with the notion of 'relational hot spots'?

- Can you apply these ideas to yourself – ground them in your own experience and may be challenge yourself around your own limiting beliefs and behaviours?

RECOMMENDED READING

Beebe and Lachmann (2002) *Infant Research and Adult Treatment: Co-constructing Interactions*. This is a book to read for a detailed account of infant research showing how relationships are co-created, and how such co-created relationships play out in later life.

Stern (1985) *The Interpersonal World of the Infant: A View from Psychoanalysis and Development Psychology*. If you are interested in research into infant development and its relevance to therapy and coaching, Stern's book is the seminal text. Though it was published some time ago it is a great book and hugely informative about how the relationship between infant and parent shapes personality development.

(Continued)

(Continued)

The ideas in this chapter have roots in the psychodynamic approach. Sandler (2011) *Executive Coaching: A Psychodynamic Approach* gives a good account of the application of this approach and will deepen and widen your understanding of the ideas presented here.

Kegan and Lahey (2009) *Immunity to Change* presents a methodology that is similar to some of the ideas in this chapter. It has become extremely popular as an approach to leadership and change, and their concept of an 'anxiety management system' perfectly expresses the key idea of a 'system of self-management' developed in this chapter.

4

Relationship Management

At the end of any session with a coachee what stays with me most is a background feeling or mood. I may be feeling excited and moved by the session, appreciative of the coachee and optimistic about the work we can do together. On other occasions I may be more downbeat, anxious or confused, maybe irritated or critical, perhaps doubting my capability as a coach. Delegates on programmes and coaches in supervision report something similar, and I anticipate that it'll be the same for you too.

Take a moment to reflect upon the coachees you've met, and imagine you're about to meet them again. Notice your feelings at the prospect – a 'something' you feel, probably in your stomach. Notice how it shifts as you bring different coachees to mind. Coaches often bring such moods to supervision, especially moods of uncertainty, anxiety and confusion. There is something happening in the coaching relationship that is hard to fathom, hard to make sense of, yet it is having an impact – an impact which is often the biggest 'take away' from the session. I am sure that this mood catches something important about the relationship which cannot yet be put into words. So what is this 'something', and how can we make sense of it? To answer these questions we need to look further into the notion of relationship management.

I said in Chapter 3 that relationship management was the other side of the coin to self-management; it is the relationship-facing side of the system of self-management. Our sense of self arises in relationship so it is here that we are at greatest risk. In relationship management I am seeking to set up a relationship with another person in which I feel safe and can operate within my 'comfort zone'. I am seeking to manage threat and anxiety by enacting a 'script' (Lapworth and Sills 2011) that I have honed from early childhood. I do this mostly outside of my conscious awareness, much as I might drive a car – skilfully, purposefully, but without giving it much deliberate thought. One way of putting this is that I have a well-rehearsed set of 'interpersonal moves', my own relational 'dance', and I invite others to join my dance, to get into step with me. Of course, we each have our own favourite dance, and how we get on together depends upon how our steps mesh. With some there is a good fit, with others there is not and we metaphorically 'step on each other's toes'. The mood I carry away from the session arises from the kind of dance we've had.

April, whom we met in Chapter 3, wanted to portray a person who is hard-working, in control and who does a good job. From her perspective, the problem was with her manager, who simply did not like her, and she'd like me to join her in this view. The invitation to join is strong, but if I simply do so (and it can be hard not to when the story is compelling) then nothing useful will happen – the same dance will continue to be played out, as we'll both agree that her manager is the problem. If I refuse to join, perhaps by insisting she attend to her part in what happens, then it's likely we'll just not 'get on' and the work will come to a halt. The challenge for me as a coach is to get alongside enough to connect with April, but be different enough to cast some light on her 'usual moves'.

In Chapter 3 we explored ways of helping April dig a bit deeper into her self-management strategies. I left the session with April carrying a kind of anxiety, wondering how she's been and whether I'd bruised her toes too much. In this chapter we are going to go further into the whole notion of relationship management because, as we'll see, this is a vital aspect of the work and it opens up possibilities that can be transformational for the coachee.

The vital nature of such work is also recognised by coachees and sponsors in organisations. The recent *Ridler Report* (based upon research compiled from about 150 sponsors of coaching in large organisations) stated that the capability to address ingrained patterns of behaviour (equivalent to our self- and relationship management) was the most important quality they wanted in a coach:

> 83% of respondents said it was 'highly important' or 'essential' for a coach to work insightfully to raise the coachee's awareness of their ingrained patterns of behaviour. This was the most highly rated option. Ingrained patterns are areas that individuals frequently do not know about themselves which have given rise to pre-programmed responses (good and bad). Once a coachee's awareness of an ingrained pattern is raised they may consider the impact their ingrained pattern has on others and whether it is a suitable way to continue to act. (Ridler & Co 2013, pp. 4–5)

To take us further into relationship management – to explore these ingrained patterns of behaviour – I'm going to introduce the concepts of transference and countertransference and then explore the concept 'use of self' as an important way of working with these patterns.

TRANSFERENCE

As mentioned in the Introduction, the concept of transference originates with Freud, and many people, whether they agree with his ideas or not, see the concept as his greatest contribution to the practical application of psychology. His account of how he came upon the concept is instructive (Freud [1912] 1978). He says that early on in his psychoanalytic practice he encountered a problem. His clients repeatedly seemed to develop strong feelings towards him, both positive and negative, which, in his view, were not merited by the kind of professional relationship that actually existed between them. Initially he took these strong feelings to be a nuisance, a hindrance to getting on with the work, something to be got out of the way. The seminal thought, which transformed psychoanalysis and much of practical psychology since then, was that these feelings, far from being a hindrance, were the recreation in the here and now of the very conflicts and issues that troubled the client and brought them to Freud in the first place. As Freud put it, the patient comes to see the analyst as 'the return, the reincarnation, of some important figures out of his childhood or past, and consequently transfers on to him feelings and reactions which undoubtedly apply to this prototype' (Freud 2010).

Significantly, the client is not aware of their experience as 'transference' – for them the feelings are real and often intense and seem to be absolutely about what is happening right now. To rather overstate it, the analyst *is* the best and most caring person they've ever met and the source of hope in the future, or *is* the most hateful and malign person imaginable.

Given this understanding, Freud shifted his view of transference from being a hindrance to it being the 'royal road' to analysis. An 'archaeological dig' into the memories of someone's past, with all their gaps, forgettings and rewritings of history, is not necessary because the impact of the past is present as transference in the analytic relationship, in all its emotional immediacy, and can be worked with in the here and now of this relationship. This transforms the potential and power of the therapeutic work, with the belief being that the conflicts and emotions worked through in the analytic relationship will in turn transform relationships in the everyday life of the client.

I hope you can see that Freud's notion of transference lines up with relationship management – or more informally, the dance the coachee invites us to join – though Freud's account catches more of the power and intensity of some of the feelings that can be present, albeit in a suppressed kind of way.

The punchline is that the way the coachee relates to others and the issues they bring to coaching are likely to reappear and be played out in the here and now of the coaching relationship, and if we can recognise them and work them through then the learning and changes can be taken back into everyday life. This way of understanding things is illustrated in Figure 4.1.

This diagram (adapted from Malan 1999) illustrates simply how patterns of relating formed early on are carried through life, and form the basis of who we are and how we get on with people in later life, including current relationships. These same patterns are taken into the coaching relationship. The question naturally arises: how do we recognise transference and then work with it? We do so as an aspect of

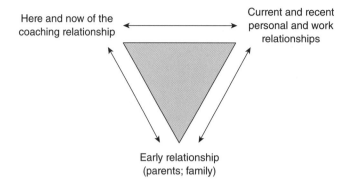

FIGURE 4.1   Triangle of relationships

developing a 'relational mindset', that is, a mindset that is consistently attuned to the significance of relationships – paying attention to the relational aspects of all we do in coaching, being alert to what is happening in the relationship, and noticing the shifts in its quality and tone.

The previous chapters have already begun the development of a relational mindset, particularly the discussions of self-management and the relational significance of contracting and boundaries. The concept of transference is a vehicle for further developing this mindset by inviting us to be interested in coachees in terms of the 'triangle of relationships': taking note of what they say about their early life and key relationships with parents, siblings, friends, teachers and what is happening in their life now, in both their work and non-work life. What we are listening for is repeating themes or patterns in relationships and then, crucially, whether there is any sense of those same themes and patterns being replayed in the coaching.

Let me introduce a new coachee to give an example of what I mean.

I have offered to do some coaching on a pro bono basis with a school, working with a number of people in their senior leadership team. I meet with Peter, who has recently become head of the English department. The school is rapidly improving but is under intense pressure to get the required GSCE results, particularly as an OFSTED inspection is expected at any time. English is a key subject and its recent results have been a cause for concern. Peter has stepped into his role at this crucial moment. As is often the case with pro bono work, there has not been a lot of attention paid to what the coaching will be about from the school, other than wanting to support and develop someone whose role is critical for the success of the academy.

At our first meeting I am struck by Peter's 'presence'. He is a diffident, reserved man, polite and quite formal. Because the contracting with the school has not been very clear he is not quite sure what coaching is or why it has been offered to him, but he has a sense that he has been chosen because there is concern about whether he is up to the job: whether he is good enough to be head of department. I invite him to tell me a bit more about himself, as a way of developing our relationship and to provide some context for our work together. It becomes clear that he has a great love of literature, of books and reading. As a boy he was always reading. He'd have a book with him in the playground at school. It was his love of books that led him to study literature at school, and then into teaching English as a profession. As he is talking, lines from the Simon and Garfunkel song 'I am a Rock' come to mind, of someone isolated and fearful of contact with others.

I ask him about teaching and how he came to take on the new post. He had been promoted internally and is struggling. He is widely recognised and appreciated as a subject specialist and it is probably on this basis that he was promoted. He loves the books, and his great desire is to get pupils interested and excited in literature. But he struggles with discipline and struggles even more with the bureaucracy of assessment, tracking pupil achievement and marking – all the things that pull him away from the subject.

His biggest concern, however, and what he wants to use the coaching for, is dealing with colleagues in the department. He is very critical of them, and doesn't think they are up to the job. As a consequence he is tending to take on more and more work, in fact taking on work others should be doing as he doesn't trust that they will do it properly. He's very stressed, feeling overwhelmed, and working evenings and weekends. I ask how he gets on with his colleagues and about the impact of this strategy on them. It becomes clear he isn't close to any of them, preferring more formal 'professional' relationships, and he doesn't know about the impact of his strategy on them.

What has my 'relational mindset' made of all this? I am struck by what he says about books in his early life, and with a sense that he is more comfortable with books than with people. More lines from the song come 'unbidden' to me as we talk, which, in terms of our discussion of self-management, suggest formidable self-protection: thick walls, a fortress; books and poetry as protection.

These lines resonate with my overall sense of him and the pattern of relating he has developed. He finds purpose, meaning and safety in literature and reading; this is his strength and the basis of his success as an English teacher. Reaching out to others is far more difficult; he finds it hard to tune into and connect with people. There is also a theme, in relation to him and others, about 'not being good enough'. The significance of all this in his current role is plain to see. Leadership is about connecting to, developing and influencing others, which runs against his way of relating to others. His pattern leads him to try to do it all himself, probably alienating others as they feel deskilled and pick up on his implied criticism of them.

I am getting a sense of the relational patterns of Peter's early life and current situation, but how is this being played out in the coaching relationship? As I said earlier, from the first moment we met I was struck by his diffidence, a formality about him which makes it hard for me to connect with him, warm to him, or enjoy working with him. I find myself thinking that this is likely to be hard work; that we are going to struggle to make contact with each other in a satisfying way (a theme which would be important for him in relation to his colleagues). There is also the theme of 'judgement': his sense that he is being 'sent' to coaching because he is not good enough, and his judgement of the capability of colleagues. This theme would become stronger as the work progressed, posing the challenge of how to invite exploration of his leadership as a positive developmental process rather than criticism and judgement of him. I also notice a sense of anxiety lurking in the background: I may not be able to help him – some sense that the onus is on me to make the coaching 'work' and I may not measure up. The anxiety of not being good enough and being judged is present for me too.

I have said that the punchline of 'transference' is working with relational patterns in the immediacy of the coaching relationship, in the belief that changes that happen here can be taken back into the outside world. With Peter, this will mean raising awareness of his diffidence, his judgementalism (of self and others) as it appears in the coaching relationship, and finding ways that we can transform our relationship so that we feel more connected and ready to learn from and not judge each other. If we can do that, then the belief is that something important will have shifted and Peter will be more able to do this with others, including colleagues in his leadership role. How we might go about this is what we'll be exploring.

TRANSFERENCE IN PRACTICE

I hope this discussion of the work with Peter has given you a more concrete understanding of transference. The concept will become clear if you can apply it to your own work. Bearing in mind the triangle of relationships, I'd like you to take some time to do the following exercise:

1. Bring to mind the coachee(s) you have been working with. If you have a number of coachees see if there is one about whom you are particularly unsure, anxious or concerned.
2. *Early life*. Write down what you know about the coachee, particularly relations with parents, siblings, other family members, friends, teachers, etc. Are there any emerging repeating themes in what you are hearing?
3. *Current and recent personal and work relationships*. Write down what you know about current relationships – with family, friends and at work. How do they get on with these people? How do they describe the kind of relationships they have with them? Is there a 'role' that is often taken up? Are there certain kinds of issues and conflicts that are present in a number of these relationships?
4. *Align (2) and (3)*. See if you can get a sense of recurrent themes and patterns in these relationships. You might, for example, be hearing repeated references to the importance of duty, of not letting people down. With April there were themes of being strong and doing a perfect job. With Peter I've noticed themes of criticism, lack of trust and self-reliance.

5. *The coaching relationship*. Now write down what has happened in the session(s) and see whether the same patterns and themes have a place in the work you are doing together. For example, in relation to coachees we have asked:

   o Is the coachee sensitive to any hint of criticism?
   o Are they being 'strong' – not showing any feelings or vulnerability?
   o Are they being 'perfect', perhaps seeking to be the perfect coachee (coming well organised to the session with topics ready to talk about; keen to report on 'homework' completed)?
   o Do they come alive when we share the books that have made a difference in our lives?

6. *Review your learning*. From the steps you have taken, see if you can integrate the themes you have noticed in the three positions of the triangle and whether this deepens your understanding of the coachee and the work you are doing together. These are the motifs at the heart of the person's sense of self and their relationships, and raising awareness of them will be fundamental to the work we'll do together. As I am sitting with the coachee I am always listening out for such themes, and I'd invite you to do the same.

There is an additional point to make about the recognition of transference and our ability to work with it. Reading about transference you might think you should be able to quickly spot the patterns, but mostly it is not like that. It often takes time to get a handle on what's going on, often only after a period of being drawn into the pattern and after the opportunity to reflect upon what has happened (primarily in supervision); hence that sense of 'Something is happening here but I don't know what it is'.

Rather than something instantly recognisable you can think of transference more in terms of a soap on television, or the plot of a film. In these scenarios we see patterns of relationships playing out over time, with different scenes and sequences of events, but behind it all there are repeating themes. For example, it is often clear that the happy excited beginning of a relationship is not going to last, particularly when we know this is the next in a long line of relationships that have not ended well. The scriptwriter is in fact working with the same basic idea we've been exploring: that people engage in repeated ingrained patterns of behaviour, which are rooted in their personal histories and shape current relationships. Another analogy is an overture at the beginning of a piece of music. All the themes that will later emerge are in the overture, in a way that portends what will unfold, but not yet in a way that can be clearly grasped. A relational mindset is attentive to the overture, listening out for the themes, and wondering about their relevance to the coaching agenda and how they will emerge in the coaching relationship.

A further point relates to how actively you attempt to find out about the coachee's life, so as to get a sense of their background and what has happened to them in the past and the present. As noted in Chapter 2, you may ask coachees to tell you something about themselves as a way of getting to know each other and providing some context for the work. I tend to ask people 'What really matters to you?' and often get a rich and heartfelt response that shifts the tenor of the session and gives a deeper insight into the relational themes we have been discussing.

I know some coaches, often working with coachees who are senior members of large organisations, who are more adventurous than I am in finding out about their coachees' lives. They might invite their coachees to do a 'life map' representing significant moments, events and people in their lives. One colleague does a 'wallet exercise', where coachees are invited to talk through the significance of the items. This exercise is often a rich source of information and insight for both coach and coachee about what is a happening in their lives, what matters, and the kinds of relationships they are involved in. It's worth pointing out that my colleague does the exercise first with his own wallet, as a way of building trust and opening the way to deepening the relationship with his coachee.

Throughout the sessions I always have my 'antenna up', listening out for relational themes in the coachee's history and what is happening now, particularly with regard to the issues brought to coaching. And I am always wondering how what is happening 'out there' is being replayed 'in here', between us in the coaching relationship.

COUNTERTRANSFERENCE

The concept of countertransference is the natural counterpoint to transference and, as we shall see, provides a doorway into a whole way of working with coachees. The concept again originates with Freud, and again it is instructive to briefly review its development over time. We shall see a similar history of initial rejection and then embracing of the idea, as another 'royal road' to practice. Freud understood countertransference as the personal reaction of the analyst to the client, the 'result of the patient's influence on (the physician's) unconscious feelings' (Freud [1910] 2001). As such, it was a danger to the neutrality required of the analyst, and Freud's prescription was that the analyst needed to have further analysis to deal with the feelings so they no longer unsettled the analytic work. Freud's strictures meant that for decades there was little written about or acknowledgement of the feelings experienced by the analyst in their work with clients.

However, in the 1950s a new view of countertransference began to emerge. A number of writers put forward the idea that the feelings evoked in the analyst had their source in the unconscious of the client (Heimann 1950; Little 1951). In other words, outside of conscious awareness, the practitioner is picking up on the feelings of the client and experiencing them as their own, and if you think about our experience in everyday life this does not seem so mysterious. I am sure you've been around someone and found that your mood changed in their presence. Feelings are stirred that are certainly my own, yet somehow I know they also say something about the person I'm with. If this is indeed the case then an important source of understanding lies closest to home – in the feelings being stirred in us by the coachee.

You'll appreciate that there are complex arguments and issues here, not least regarding how the analyst (or any practitioner) understands and manages the ambiguity of the source of feelings. Indeed, there has been an enormous amount written on the subject, exploring it in great depth and subtlety. Nevertheless, the weight of opinion has shifted more and more to the view that the countertransference – or what I might call the practitioner's 'self-experience' – has a vital role to play in understanding and working with coachees.

The 'relational turn' in therapy has provided its own way of understanding countertransference. If the coachee brings their patterns of relating into the room (which is the relational understanding of transference) then it follows that the coach will feel the impact of those patterns. How will that impact be registered? The answer to this has already been given, in part, at the beginning of this chapter. It is registered as a mood, feelings or, to use Gendlin's (2003) term, a 'felt sense' that is evoked in the coach in the presence of the coachee. I strongly believe that present in this feeling is the 'story' of what is happening in the coaching relationship, which I'll not truly be able to grasp through simply thinking about the situation, but can grasp through paying attention to and 'unpacking' the 'felt sense'. I may also register the impact through things that come 'unbidden' to mind, such as the lines of a song or particular memories (where the memories have a resonance with something that is happening in the coaching relationship).

Let's return to my coachee Peter, to see how this applies in practice. One thing is immediately obvious: the lines of the song that came to me were significant. As I see it, those lines have gathered up a deep 'intuitive' sense of Peter, an intuition based on everything about his manner and our meeting so far. I also need to acknowledge an affinity with Peter, and those lines, as I recognise similarities between us. It has been a favourite song of mine, poignantly catching themes in my life. So who do the lines 'belong to', Peter or me? Well, both of us I think. They resonate with my life and, I believe, his too. What do I do with those lines – do I share them with him? Well, no; at least not now. Our relationship has not developed sufficiently to make such sharing useful or appropriate. I am also aware of their resonance with me, so I want to take care and allow more time for me to get a secure sense of their relevance to his life. At the same time, I see the lines as a rich and probably quite accurate source of understanding, and with this comes a sense of compassion and connection with him. I have a sense of the depth of his anxiety and the magnitude of the challenge he faces if he is to make the necessary changes.

What is my 'felt sense' during and after the session? It's hard to articulate, and I realise I don't want to 'go there', as I don't like it. As I mentioned earlier, there is a kind of anxiety. Staying with that feeling, what emerges is a sense of not being good enough; that the work is too difficult and I'm not quite up to it; that I am going to disappoint. So what do I make of all this? First, I know that it is important to stay with and pay attention to this felt sense even though I'd rather move on and do something else. And I'm sure at times you'll have similar experiences in your coaching – that feeling in the background, like bad news, that you'd rather not hear. So my message to you is stay with it, sit with it: it will be worth it.

Staying with and focusing further on my felt sense, I realise that the work is going to be a real challenge. Given the pressures and the timescale Peter may not be able to make the necessary changes, and in this sense there is a reality to the feeling that I may well 'not be good enough' and disappoint. It may be, of course, that what emerges from the work is that Peter has found himself on the wrong path, that the career in teaching is taking him further and further along a route that is profoundly wrong for him, and this becomes the real issue.

There is another dimension to all this, however, which is of great significance. There is the possibility that my felt sense resonates with Peter's own deeper anxieties and fears – his belief that he is not good enough, will disappoint and fail, both in relation to taking on the role of head of department but also, as intuitively grasped in the lines to the song, in life in general. The realisation of this possibility reorientates my whole sense of that feeling; I feel a shift and kind of relief along with a sense of having grasped something deeper about our work together. This new understanding does not spell out to me what I should do about all this, but I feel ready to re-engage with Peter, having shifted that background sense of not being good enough, which reinforces the growing sense of compassion for him and a desire to do my best by him.

COUNTERTRANSFERENCE IN PRACTICE

As with transference, countertransference will become more real to you if you can connect with it in relation to your own work. I'd like you to return to one of the coachees you focused on in the exercise on transference, but this time:

- Bring to mind the coachee and the session you had together. Recall how the work started, how the session went, and how you were as you left the session. Take your time over this; let yourself reconnect with the session.
- Now relax, make yourself comfortable and imagine you are about to meet the coachee again. Do this as concretely as possible: visualise the building; who else you might meet; the sounds; the smell – take yourself to that place. Now you are about to meet them, what is the feeling evoked in you? What is that 'felt sense' in your body?
- Sit with that feeling, hold it in focus and see if a word, image, lines from a song or something else comes up that seems to resonate with that feeling, that makes

it meaningful to you. It may be that a word or image arises that nearly but not quite catches the meaning. Stay with it and see if something comes that resonates. You'll know if you've got it as you'll feel a shift in yourself, something like a sense of relief (like when you finally get a name that you haven't quite been able to recall).

- Now ask yourself what that feeling says about you and the coachee and the work you are doing together. What new understanding do you have?
- Bring the earlier exercise on transference and this exercise on countertransference together. How does your 'felt sense' deepen your understanding of what you've already gleaned about the coachee and their way of being in the world?

USE OF SELF

'Self-experience' is the expression I'm using to refer to the thoughts, feelings and behaviours that arise in the coach in relation to the coachee. I have been exploring this self-experience under the heading of countertransference, drawing upon the psychodynamic tradition, but other approaches have their own terms for the same thing. For example, the person-centred approach has the concept of congruence, whilst gestalt has the notion of 'use of self'. The questions arise: What is the place of self-experience in coaching? What are the issues, and how might self-experience be used? More specifically, should I share with the coachee – should I disclose my self-experience?

It seems fair to say that, for many people new to coaching, self-experience has no place at all. Initially the proposition that my own feelings are relevant to the work seems strange and rather alarming. Indeed, for some, such self-experience hardly seems to exist as they are so used to 'looking outwards' rather than 'inwards' that the first challenge is to begin to attend to themselves and notice what is there. For those who come to coaching from this position, paying attention to self and realising its potential in relationships can be a revelation, both personally and professionally.

What is your starting place around self-experience?

- Do you notice what is arising in you in everyday life in your relations with others – that 'felt sense' that is present in the background of all relationships?
- What do you make of the proposition that such self-experience is important in coaching?
- What are your thoughts about sharing that experience with coachees?

Peter Bluckert's statement brings all of these questions into sharp focus: 'I regard the use of self as *the* highest order coaching skill. It can be the difference between good and great coaching' (Bluckert 2006, p. 84). As you can see, Bluckert argues that the capability to use that self-experience, that felt sense, is the highest of coaching skills, and I agree with him. As such, it's important to go into the issues and possibilities in a bit more detail.

Use of self brings an active connotation to self-experience – how I will use it when working with coachees. Gestalt practitioners also sometimes refer to this as 'self as instrument'. There is a certain mechanical or mechanistic feel to the words that do not appeal to me; nevertheless, the expression has become common currency and catches that active sense of using self-experience, so we'll stay with it.

Let me lay out three positions on what we might call a 'spectrum of use of self' in relation to self-experience:

1. Misguided and damaging.
2. Useful data but not directly shared.
3. Vital and integral to practice.

1. MISGUIDED AND DAMAGING

This position harks back to Freud's strictures about countertransference. In this view self-experience is purely personal; it is just the coach's personal reactions to the coachee and the issues they are bringing to the session. At best it will only confuse matters if I take the view that my experience is somehow attributable to the coachee; at worst I may project onto the coachee all my unresolved personal issues.

For instance, in my work with Peter I am quite clear that the lines 'I am a rock; I am an island' have a strong resonance with my own life. On what basis do I attribute to Peter something clearly to do with my own life? How can I disentangle what belongs to me from what belongs to Peter? I'm sure you'll see the strength of this argument. As it stands, we are not yet in a position to fully respond to these arguments. We will need to come back to this issue once we have looked more closely into the coach's contribution to the relationship.

2. USEFUL DATA BUT NOT DIRECTLY SHARED

This position gives credence to the proposition that other people have an impact on us that we register emotionally and intuitively, but there is a reticence to sharing directly this experience with the coachee as there is the danger of intruding into the coachee's work, disrupting its own flow and direction. What I can do, however, is use what is evoked in me as a source of data that give me possible insights into the coachee, maybe forming hypotheses that orientate my listening and can be checked along the way by what then transpires (Sandler 2011).

This is what happened with Peter: 'I am a rock; I am an island' is potentially a rich source of understanding for me. I can now listen out to what else he says that can confirm, fine-tune or maybe discount that understanding. I may also ask some questions that are guided by that view, fully ready to let go of it if it seems to be on the wrong track. For example, with Peter – and given the coaching agenda we have agreed about working more effectively with colleagues – I might ask him questions about how he relates to his co-workers. Does he share his concerns with them? Does he seek their views? Does he offer them support or challenges? The kind of presence he has and the lines from the song suggest to me that he is unlikely to do any of these things, although their relevance to his coaching agenda is obvious. My question to him about the impact of his strategy on his colleagues is a way of testing out my emerging view, and beginning to raise awareness around these themes. His answer suggests that I am on the right track.

3. VITAL AND INTEGRAL TO PRACTICE

This position puts the use of self at the centre of practice. The discussion of relational patterns, transference and countertransference has given a rationale for believing that self-experience is significant, but we've not yet posed the question of whether and how it might be disclosed to coachees. We have a flavour as to the strong arguments for not disclosing – the inappropriate intrusion of the coach's personal material into the coaching – but what are the arguments for use of self?

There are two distinct but overlapping strands here. The first might be termed 'technical', to do with the power and impact of such disclosure and how to do it in practice. The second might be termed 'relational', and concerns the impact of use of self on the quality and depth of the relationship. Let's take a closer look at these two strands and what this might all look like in practice.

THE TECHNICAL ASPECT OF USE OF SELF

I think it's important that we first get clear about **what** might be disclosed. It's not advice, guidance or suggestions that come to mind during the session, nor is it a sharing of personal history or recounting of experiences that are similar to the coachee's. As has been indicated, it is more about the reactions that come up whilst working with the coachee – reactions that are often more background than fore-ground, a kind of feeling, mood or felt sense rather than something clear and easily articulated. If you are a visual person it may be an image that comes up or, as happened with Peter and me, the lines from a song. All these examples have one quality – they come 'unbidden', they arrive and may 'settle in'. There is often another quality, but their meaning isn't clear. Sharing it can therefore feel a bit risky, as I don't know how meaningful it is or whether the coachee will connect with it. Some examples may help to clarify this:

- I am working with Jenny, who is telling a very positive story. She is very bright and pleased with her new job. I am pleased for her too, but in the background I notice something else in me, a kind of sadness or upset that persists and which I cannot make sense of. I share my pleasure at how well things are going and then add that 'There is something else around for me, which I don't understand, a kind of sadness or upset. Does this have any meaning for you?' It does and she becomes quite tearful. She knows the new job is a great opportunity and she should be grateful it has come her way. But she has had to move away from family and friends and set up a new home. She feels lonely and homesick, but doesn't think she has the right to say so.
- I have just started working with John. He is on a leadership development programme where all the participants are offered coaching. We have been through the initial contracting phase and he has started to talk about one of his coaching topics. He has plenty to say, but I notice a disconnection in me, a kind of boredom as he speaks. It feels a bit risky but I say to him something like: 'There seems to be a kind of lack of energy here as we are speaking. Do you know what I mean?' He smiles and gives me a bit more background. He is sceptical about the whole notion of coaching, but has come along because it would look bad if he didn't. He too has a sense of 'going through the motions'. We now have the real agenda, which we need to deal with if we are going to work together. I'm not bored or disconnected now, and neither is he.

How might this look with Peter? I've said that I'd probably not share the lines from the song that came up early on, as they are evocative of a deep and personal experience and I don't think our relationship is ready to enter that territory yet. If, however, we do build a sense of trust, and if they are still with me when we are talking more deeply about how he relates to others, including his colleagues at work, I might share the lines with him. I might confess that they are meaningful to me, but say that they've come to mind when we've been working together. Does he know the song? Does it have a special meaning for him? My hunch is that he'll say yes to both questions. How about the felt sense of not being good enough, of failing and being a disappointment? Early on I might draw on that feeling to share a sense of the size and importance of the role he has taken on and the challenges this presents to him. Later, if trust builds, I might more directly share the anxiety I notice about being good enough and invite curiosity as to what it might mean.

USE OF SELF: WHEN AND HOW?

What guidelines can be offered about the use of self?

- First, it is something that arises in the session – a feeling, image or intuition – and does so as something 'unbidden'.
- Although it is sometimes quite prominent, it is more often a background sense, something present but easily overlooked – especially if it is something I find discomforting.
- Most often I don't know what that feeling means. It may seem at odds with the general tenor of the session. It may be that we are focusing on the issue the coachee has brought, talking about the details of the situation, when I notice its (probably unobtrusive) presence, which I cannot fathom.
- Work with the proposition that this 'something', though definitely mine, may be about what is happening in the relationship between us.
- Share whatever it is with the coachee, in a way that invites curiosity and interest about its meaning and relevance to the session. You'll see in the two earlier examples that I share the feeling without explicitly saying 'this is my feeling', though this is clearly implied. In my wording, ownership of the feeling is left unstated, hanging between us, and I invite the coachee to check their own connection with it. If you try this I'm sure you'll be surprised at how often the coachee picks up and works with what you say. Placing the feeling 'between us' without explicitly owning it is a method I've developed when working with use of self. More often, and just as effectively, I've seen coaches explicitly own the feeling, perhaps saying something like: 'As we are talking I notice in me a kind of upset or sadness. Have you any sense of that too?' With practice you'll find the way of working that suits you.
- Find the words that the coachee can connect with and use rather than being confused or put off. I normally try to be quite direct and descriptive of what I am experiencing. With Jenny I speak of **sadness** or **upset**, which directly described my experience. On occasions, when the feeling may be more difficult to share, I may be more circumspect. With John I did not say 'I am bored', but rather 'There seems to be a lack of energy here', which expressed my sense of what was happening in a way John could 'hear' and respond to. There may be times when something more direct is needed. Lietaer (1993) recounts Carl Rogers saying that if he is bored he thinks it is better he says it – knowing that he'll not be bored once he has said it.
- In supervision I've heard coaches express directly how they are feeling (perhaps being bored) as a direct – and as they see it much needed – challenge to the coachee. Such challenging interventions have their place but have to be handled with care. My recommendation to you, particularly as you begin with use of

self, is to find the words that invite curiosity and collaborative exploration of the meaning of what you have shared.

- Use of self often feels a bit risky as the coachee can easily discount any connection with what you say, disclaiming its relevance to them. When this happens (which I find is surprisingly rare) I tend not to pursue it and accept it may just be me, or perhaps just 'park it' for now with the possibility that something important is being addressed but we are not ready to go into it. If it is significant it will persist or return.

As remarked earlier, Bluckert says that use of self is the highest-order coaching skill and you can probably see why. It requires self-awareness on your part, the capacity to tune into yourself during the session, notice what is there, and share this with the coachee in a way they can hear and work with. The good news is that I repeatedly see people on courses trying out use of self in practice sessions and discovering that it 'works', that they can do it, and that it frequently transforms the sessions – in direction and depth. Of course, as with any skill it develops with practice, but I invite you to try it out and see what happens.

THE RELATIONAL ASPECT OF USE OF SELF

As a I coach I'm not taking a neutral stance regarding my coachees; rather I am 'on their side', wanting them to achieve whatever they want to achieve, and I am doing this in part through the kind of models, concepts and skills we have been discussing. Use of self adds something more to the mix. Through it I'm bringing myself more into the relationship, showing more of myself, being touched by what is happening – maybe feeling sad, upset, excited or inspired.

I cannot help but notice a shift in myself as I recognise and say these things. I am becoming more involved and letting the coachee know that. It may be that this adds to the sense of risk that often accompanies use of self. It seems to challenge the usual professional stance – that separate, 'expert' manner. Use of self takes me to the edge, to the frontier of the personal–professional divide, and sets up a profound challenge. How do I bring myself, as me, into the relationship **and** stay professional? Where is the line? How do I know if and when I'm crossing it? Indeed, it puts me up against the challenges of authenticity: can I be myself, be open and honest with myself and the coachee, **and** be professional?

There is no 'right answer' here. Each person will find their own position, though the professional boundaries are marked out by our codes of ethics. My own experience has been that the more I allow myself to enter fully into the relationship the greater the depth of the work. The more I care for the coachee the more they matter to me, and the more I show that this is the case the better the work tends to be. As I enter more deeply into the relationship the use of self tends to shift from 'technique' to a genuine sharing of what is going on for me. We are now deeply into the questions about the coaching relationship, because I know that attitudes towards some coachees involve a sense of care, concern, looking forward to meeting them and pleasure in their company – emotions can run quite deep and they are not separate to the quality of the work we do together. Quite the opposite: it is here that the best work can happen.

I'm sure you'll see, however, that such personal involvement brings its own anxieties. You may be experiencing that right now as you read this. Where is that line between the personal and the professional? I know you too will have to confront this question, this dilemma. There is no 'view from nowhere' and it is not possible to take a neutral position, because that is a stance in itself. For me the bottom line in all of this, or rather what draws the line, is that my involvement, if it is to remain professional, has be about the welfare of the coachee and honouring the agreement we have reached about the purpose of the coaching. Bearing this in mind is what helps keep me the right side of the line.

PRESENCE

The diagram of self- and relationship management makes it clear that both parties in a relationship co-create their relationship, and this applies in coaching as elsewhere. The discussion of use of self has put the focus on what you as the coach bring into the coaching relationship as you share your self-experience. Of course, what you bring to the relationship is more than use of self. You bring your whole 'way of being': your strategies of self- and relationship management; your professional experience and know-how; your cultural background and so forth. This 'way of being' has been described as the kind of 'presence' (Nevis 1997; Rainey Tolbert and Hanafin 2006) we have in relationships. For example, my presence may be mostly calm and thoughtful, or restless and energetic, or perhaps somewhat detached and analytic. You often get a sense of someone's presence from the very first moment you meet them and this can form the basis of how we then interact with them.

For the most part people tend to be unaware of the kind of presence they have, as it is the background 'way of being' in the world. They will also tend to be unaware of the kind of impact their presence has on others and how this contributes to the co-creation of the relationship. A calm, thoughtful presence has a different impact to a restless energetic presence. One way of describing much of what we've been discussing about coaching is that we are seeking to raise the coachee's awareness of the kind of presence they have and its impact on others.

A challenge for you as a coach is to become aware of the kind of presence you have and its likely impact on the coachees with whom you work. A further challenge then arises: are you able to flex your presence to provide the kind of presence needed in the particular coaching relationship? For example, you may have a calm, receptive presence which enables the coachee to feel safe, accepted and ready to share sensitive material. However you may need a different, more provocative presence at times to raise the coachee's awareness of their contribution to events (Nevis 1997). Each of us tends to have a 'default' kind of presence; the challenge is to become aware of that presence and to widen our range of ways of being with others.

IMPLICATIONS FOR PRACTICE

This chapter completes the cycle of self and relationship regulation. Do you find this framework useful to you, particularly the aspect we've looked at here of self-management?

To make the concepts of transference and countertransference more real I recommend you consider them in relation to your own life:

- Do you recognise ingrained patterns of behaviour in your own life, which have their roots in childhood and are very present in your current work and non-work life?
- Do you have a sense of the kind of relationships you feel most comfortable with and how you may invite others to 'get in step' with you?

Apply the concepts to your coachees:

- Listen for themes in their work.
- Try out the triangle of relationships.
- Notice the 'felt sense' or mood both during and after sessions, and explore its meaning in the coaching relationship.
- Consider how you might use countertransference, and try out use of self with your coachees.
- What kind of presence do you think you have?
- What kind of impact does your presence have on others?
- What kind of impact does it having in coaching?
- What kind of presence would 'widen the range' of what you currently offer?

RECOMMENDED READING

I strongly recommend that you buy and read Gendlin (2003) *Focusing: How to Gain Direct Access to Your Body's Knowledge: How to Open Up Your Deeper Feelings and Intuition*. It is a small, easily readable 'manual' about how to recognise and gain meaning from the 'felt sense', which is the tacit background feeling I've been referring to throughout the chapter. There is also a lot of material available online on 'focusing' and 'felt sense', including video demonstrations of the technique.

Yalom (2002) *The Gift of Therapy* is a gem. Don't be put off by the title. He is an exceptionally gifted writer and there is a lot in here directly applicable to coaching, particularly the chapters on disclosure and working in the here and now. He gives lots of practical examples that are invaluable.

If you'd like to read more on transference, particularly a critique of the concept, then I highly recommend Szasz (1963) 'The concept of transference', *International Journal of Psychoanalysis*. He offers a powerful critique of some of the assumptions and possible misuses of transference.

If you would like to read more on use of self, there are the following books and journal papers: Wosket (1999) *The Therapeutic Use of Self: Counselling Practice, Research and Supervision*; Rowan and Jacobs (2002) *The Therapist's Use of Self*; Rainey Tolbert and Hanafin (2006) 'Use of self in OD consulting: what matters is presence', in B. Jones and M. Brazzel (eds), *The NTL Handbook of Organization Development and Change*; Baldwin (2000) *The Use of Self in Therapy*.

5

Widening the Field

The focus of Chapters 3 and 4 has been on the psychological dimension of the coach, the coachee and the relationship between them. This dimension sits within a wider context to which we must now turn, because coaching cannot adequately be understood as an abstraction from the relationships within which it is embedded. This context and these relationships have, I would argue, a particular quality; they are interconnected, interwoven, and particular 'figures' (e.g. a coaching agenda) cannot adequately be addressed without raising awareness of their 'ground', i.e. the totality of relationships of which they are a part. This totality can be named in various ways. In the next chapter we'll explore it under the heading of culture. In this chapter we'll explore it through the notion of 'field' and through an extended example of how you can make the field very apparent when working with a client. We'll then draw upon an existential perspective to further deepen our appreciation of the significance of emotion, or 'affect' in coaching. We'll conclude the chapter by drawing attention to an important related concept, that of 'system'.

FIELD THEORY

The notion of field has its roots in the work of Kurt Lewin (Parlett 1991; 1997), and is an important strand of the gestalt approach. Lewin took the concept of field from physics – magnetic, electrical, gravitational fields – and with it the understanding that the properties of anything in a field can only be understood in terms of the field as a whole. He applied this principle to human behaviour:

> Whether or not a certain type of behaviour occurs depends not on the presence or absence of one fact or a number of facts viewed in isolation, but upon the constellation (the structure and forces) of the specific field as a whole. The 'meaning' of the single fact depends upon its position in the field. (Lewin 1952, p. 150)

The concept of field invites us to attend to the interrelatedness of all that we are involved with, and the understanding that the meaning of any particular aspect (relationship, event, behaviour) is conditioned by the total situation. This total situation includes the past and future:

> the psychological past and the psychological future are simultaneously parts of the psychological field at any given time. The time perspective is continually changing. According to field theory, any type of behaviour depends upon the total field, including the time perspective at that time but not, **in addition**, upon any past or future field and its time perspective. (Lewin 1952, p. 54, emphasis added)

Lewin coined the phrase 'life-space' to characterise the field of any particular individual. From a field perspective we have to attend to the 'total situation' (life-space) of coach and coachee, including their past histories and future plans, goals and ambitions. But these past and future aspects are not to be considered as separate, distinct realms (e.g. history 'explaining' current behaviour) but rather as aspects of the present, here-and-now, field.

The notion of field has a strong resonance with our discussion in Chapter 1 of the gestalt theory of perception, with its focus on meaning arising from the whole 'perceptual field' (rather than particular stimuli within the field) and how a particular figure emerges from its ground. These three concepts of field, figure and ground provide valuable resources for understanding the coaching process and coaching relationship:

- The coachee brings issues to discuss, often framed as 'goals', which are figural for the coachee in the session (e.g. time management, difficulties with a manager, future career, work–life balance).
- From a field perspective, such figures are understood not as separate, self-contained issues but as interwoven with and emerging from the 'ground' of the coachee's life-space.
- The coach seeks to enable the coachee to attend to the place of the figural issue within the wider field through the process of raising awareness, and in so doing enables new figures, new meanings, to emerge, which become the basis for new possibilities of action.
- The coaching relationship is understood as a field that is co-created through the coming-together of the life-space of both parties, a unique constellation that is constantly changing (for example, the decision by the coach to try out a new model or skill that they've learned on their coaching programme).

There are a number of complex ideas here. Let's see what they might look like in practice. Adrian, the coach, meets with Barbara, a member of a senior leadership team in a large accountancy business. Barbara wants to talk about her relationship with the CEO, Rebecca, as she feels disconnected from her, with little influence around key decisions. Her goal in the coaching is to improve her relationship with Rebecca so as to have more influence on decisions. Adrian has been learning about 'creative approaches' to coaching, including using objects to 'sculpt' the coachee's issues, and is looking for an opportunity to try this out. He suggests to Barbara that she takes some of the objects he has brought along (figures, objects, stones) and map out the situation as she talks about it. In doing this they are, in effect, mapping the field.

Barbara chooses a small shiny stone to represent herself. She then picks up a much larger stone to represent Rebecca, and places it some distance away. Next she picks three figures to represent the other members of the senior leadership team, and the figures she selects prove to be very significant. One figure is a mechanical man, another a sheep, and the third a tiger. Though Barbara had initially said her issue was with the CEO, she spends considerable time talking through her relationships with each of these colleagues, since each of them separately, and together as members of the team, have an important part to play in 'configuring the field'. You can probably catch some of the flavour of what she said about the 'mechanical man' and the 'sheep' simply by the figures themselves. However, Barbara paid particular attention to her relationship to John, head of HR, who appears as the tiger. She realises she is terrified of him. She has seen him 'maul' other people, and so keeps her distance from him, and keeps quiet and never challenges his views in leadership team meetings. See Figure 5.1.

In 'sculpting the field', it becomes obvious that the three other members of the leadership team stand 'between' her and the CEO, and that she will need to find her proper place in the team if she is to have any real connection with Rebecca. This is a daunting prospect, particularly dealing with her relationship with John.

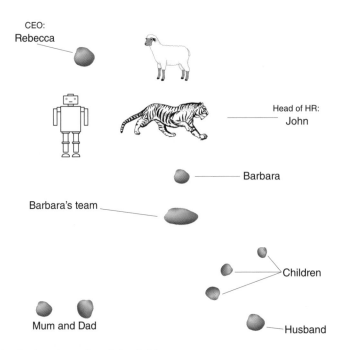

FIGURE 5.1   Barbara's sculpt of the field

Adrian had invited Barbara to use the objects to map the field, and as she spoke different people became figural, each configuring the field anew as the network of relationships became more complex. The meaning of Barbara's relationship with Rebecca made sense *within* that network, a field that was also configured by Barbara's past (e.g. how she typically dealt with conflict) and her future (the intention to be successful in her post).

As tends to be the way, however, through the very process of awareness raising, more of the 'ground' came into view. Without deliberately setting out to do so, Barbara found herself reaching for more objects to represent her husband and their children, and also her mum and dad. She was surprised, indeed somewhat shocked, to see that she placed her husband behind their three children (somewhat reminiscent of how the CEO is placed behind the other members of the leadership team). She could also see that her relationship with her own team at work was 'between' her and her family. A new figure emerged strongly: work was masking some serious difficulties with her husband which she did not want to face. Indeed, she came to wonder whether the focus on her relationship with Rebecca was a form of self-protection from something even more disturbing – the state of her relationships at home.

The field is becoming more complex, and in future sessions it becomes more so. For example, the relationship with her elderly parents becomes figural; they are becoming frail and nearing the point where they won't be able to live without more support. Adrian invites Barbara to sculpt how she would like the relation-ships (the field) to be in the future, and the whole constellation is reconfigured (including Barbara having chosen a bigger stone to represent herself).

We can see from this example how Barbara's stated issue is, in fact, a field issue, involving a complex network of relationships, and that successfully addressing the relationship with the CEO is likely to involve consideration of those other rela-tionships. In fact, the whole nature of the issue can be recast from the field perspective. In this instance, the real challenge for Barbara may be in her relations with the senior leadership team members and perhaps, at an even deeper level, the relationship with her husband.

This example of Barbara is entirely typical of what frequently happens in coaching, and why the notion of field is so apt. Coachees come with a particular concern that may seem quite clear and distinct. However, as we explore further, other facets of the situation come into view which can transform the whole scene. These other facets, from a distance, might seem separate and distinct, but closer attention reveals the interconnectedness; they are all part of the same picture, the same field. Widening the field draws in the bigger picture and allows us to grasp the deeper underlying issues.

Also, of course, though we have only hinted at it, the coach's 'field' also co-constructs the conversation. We mentioned at the beginning of this example that the coach is trying out a new 'technique' of using objects to sculpt the coachee's situation. This introduces a very different way of making sense of the coachee's agenda. It also has a powerful impact on the nature of the conversation itself, as coach and coachee shift from a face-to-face conversation to shared interest and enquiry about the sculpt, what this 'shows up' and how it might be different. You can imagine for yourself how using different models, skills and techniques will refashion the field of the coaching relationship, as well as factors such as the confidence of the coach, the setting for the session, whether the coach and coachee have mutual acquaintances (it might be that Barbara was referred to Adrian through a colleague whom they both know well) and so on.

THE FIELD: A 'BREADTH PSYCHOLOGY'

Chapters 4 and 5, on self- and relationship management, offered what could loosely be described as a 'depth psychology' in the sense that the coachee's current behaviour is understood in terms of the influence of their early life. The field generates an additional psychological dimension, which I've termed, again very loosely, a 'breadth psychology' – how our sense of self is interwoven with the here-and-now configuration of the field, the current network of relationships.

In our example Barbara's sense of identity as a member of a senior leadership team, and as a mother, wife and daughter, is formed in the field and will shift as the field shifts. To take one aspect, her concerns over the well-being of her ageing parents is to do with their increasing frailty, and her hopes, fears and behaviours will change as their situation changes; or again, the challenges she has with the senior leadership team are, in some measure, evoked by the characters in the team and the particular culture they co-create – the sheep, the mechanical man and the tiger that mauls. Her feelings, what she is thinking and how she is behaving will change with the shifting dynamics of the team. From this perspective self is, in some measure, a field phenomenon.

There is no doubt that 'depth psychology' (self- and relationship management strategies) and 'breadth psychology' (arising from the dynamics of the field) are interwoven, but as we have seen, each dimension has its own dynamics and has to be taken into account. Barbara's reaction to John is rooted in her own history but that's not the full story; other people are also frightened of and avoid John. Empathy is so powerful precisely because it is a way of gathering together both the depth and breadth psychologies: to stand in the other's shoes and get a sense of their field. I'm sure you can stand for a moment in Barbara's shoes and get a feel for her concerns about her parents.

FEELINGS, EMOTIONS AND MOOD FROM THE PERSPECTIVE OF FIELD

In previous chapters we've repeatedly returned to the subject of feelings and emotion, and explored the vital part they play in coaching. There is an even deeper aspect for us now to consider, when we understand 'affect' from a field perspective.

You'll notice that 'mood' has been added to this section's heading (alongside 'feelings' and 'emotions'). This is because there is something particular about mood that is important in our discussion. What's the difference between emotion and mood? They are closely related, overlapping concepts, but a primary difference is that feeling and emotion usually refer to more well-defined states with specific situations or objects as their trigger, whereas mood is often harder to define with a source or reference that is less clear. For example, I am angry, excited or sad about something, maybe about a forthcoming specific event (a wedding, a football match, a meeting at work), so both emotion and its reference are relatively clear. On the other hand, I may find myself ill at ease and unsure why this is so; more 'in a mood' which I don't quite understand. Though often harder to pin down than feeling and emotion, we shall see that attending to mood opens up new possibilities for coaching.

I mentioned in the Introduction that the existential approach of Martin Heidegger has profoundly affected my practice, and it is his analysis of mood and emotion that is the basis of the ideas we'll explore here. In some extraordinary pages in *Being and Time* (Heidegger 1962, pp. 172–82) he challenges the taken-for-granted Western view that moods and emotion are primarily the personal subjective experience of self-contained individuals, and argues instead that they are a fundamental aspect of the shared social/cultural situation: something we find ourselves 'in' as an aspect of our 'being in the world', or, to use the language of this chapter, as an aspect of the field.

I've tried to capture something of this approach in the modification of our basic diagram in Figure 5.2. Rather than closed circles for self and other, they're represented as 'open systems' permeated by mood, which is the shared ground of the relationship – a relationship which itself is embedded in a wider cultural/organisational field. In this view mood is continually circulating between self and other in the shared field.

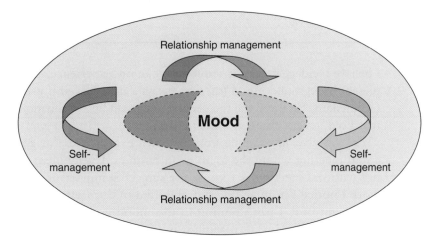

FIGURE 5.2 Mood: personal but not just personal

THE INTELLIGENCE OF MOOD AND MOTION

> Mood always has its understanding ... Understanding always has its mood. (Heidegger 1962, p. 182)

In Heidegger's view, mood and emotion are not just pure 'feelings' or 'affect'. They are always permeated by meaning; they always contain an understanding of the world. Similarly, any understanding of the world is not purely cognitive; it also has its own mood. For example, a memorial service has both mood and meaning, which inform each other. Heidegger takes another step, arguing that mood and emotion contain a deeper understanding of the world than that which is possible by thinking alone: 'the possibilities of disclosure which belong to cognition reach far too short a way compared with the primordial disclosure belonging to moods' (ibid., p.173).

This is somewhat controversial stuff – how can mood 'disclose' (i.e. reveal) the world more than cognition? After all, in the traditional view, mood, emotion and feelings are purely subjective and personal states; indeed they are 'irrational', thus by definition not rational, and not to be trusted. In this view, when clear thinking is needed, emotion must be controlled. This takes us back to our original discussion of emotion: the danger of opening up Pandora's box and emotions being 'allowed out'.

Take some time to consider the proposition that mood and emotion are a source of understanding – a source of 'data':

- Can you bring to mind occasions when what you are feeling, your mood, is a source of understanding ('data'), about the people and situation that you are involved with?
- Have you had occasions when your emotion/mood has proved to be a better guide than your thinking?

I believe Heidegger is right about mood. In my experience attending to that ever-present background mood (there is always a mood, even if it is one of disinterest or boredom) has given me the deepest understanding of situations – understanding that I did not get through thinking alone.

Let me give an example from my own experience. I'm going into work, to a staff meeting where the focus is on business development. I'm up for engaging with the meeting as I know the subject is important. However, as I get to work I notice I'm in an odd mood – kind of dissociated; present but somehow a little out of it. I pay attention to this mood using Gendlin's (2003) 'focusing' approach, and an image/metaphor jumps out at me: 'a computer in safe mode'.

I immediately know this is right; the metaphor has perfectly caught the meaning of the mood I'm in. Though at the level of conscious intent I'm ready for the meeting, the reality is that we are all already working at a fast pace and this is taking its toll both physically and mentally. To add more business development at this time is potentially hazardous and somehow I know this, not cognitively but in my mood, which has been symbolised and made meaningful by the image. A computer goes into safe mode when something is not right; something may be damaging, and the computer closes down much of its capacity and potential in order to remain safe – just as I notice a kind of dissociation in me. At the beginning of the meeting I share my mood, the image and my understanding of it. You'll not be surprised to hear that my mood catches the mood of others – though because mood tends to be in the background it would be so easy to ignore and just get on with the agenda. However, on this occasion, and by attending to the mood, the agenda shifts to a review of what is happening in the business and what we – and the business – really need.

There are a number of points we can draw out of this example:

- I did not choose to be in the mood: it came 'unbidden' and 'had me' whether I wanted it or not.
- The mood had a better understanding than my conscious thinking about the situation, and I find this to be typical, such that I now always attend to my mood as well as my thinking: the trick is to give the mood proper focus and space to allow its meaning to become evident.
- The mood was personal but not just personal: *about me but also about the situation*. This is a vital new point with huge significance for coaching – the coachee's mood and emotion are personal to them but also an aspect of a shared field; it contains an understanding of the situation, an understanding that goes deeper than that available to thinking alone.
- This account of mood provides a theoretical basis for understanding the dynamics of transference, countertransference and use of self, viewing us as open systems registering the realities of the situations and relationships with which we are involved, but registering this at the level of mood and emotion. From this perspective use of self makes sense, as it is rooted in the same mood/emotional field as the coachee and, via the coachee, their organisation.
- I'm equating Gendlin's (2003) 'felt sense' to mood, and on that basis find his 'focusing' a powerful way of attending to and finding the meaning in mood. The good news is that we've already put felt sense and focusing centre stage in our discussion of use of self, so we have a ready-made way of working with mood. The key, to repeat, is to attend to both aspects of mood: personal but not just personal – mood is data about the coachee *and* their situation.

Heidegger's approach to mood and emotion can be surprising when encountered from the perspective of the individual. It becomes more obvious, even commonplace, when encountered from a field perspective. It is commonplace to speak of 'the mood of the nation', and we've all experienced the 'mood' of a meeting, group, team or organisation, particularly that moment of first joining and knowing that the mood that 'hits us' tells us more about what is happening than is being put into words; that the mood has 'intelligence' of what is really going on, even if the overt behaviour conveys a different message. Such experience makes sense of the notion that we are open systems, part of an emotional field that is personally felt but not just personal.

MOOD AND EMOTION AS AN 'ATTUNEMENT' TO THE WORLD

Heidegger's word for mood is *Stimmung*, which can also be translated into English as 'attunement'. Attunement has various connotations, such as being in harmony, resonance and being 'in tune', connotations that have their basis in music and catch the sense of 'shared vibration' between separate elements – for example the harmony of a choir. A strong metaphor for me is a tuning fork and the reciprocal influence between the fork and its field, where they both resonate together. The power of such resonance can have surprising effects. For example, the Albert Bridge in London has a sign dating from 1873 warning soldiers to break step as they cross, because of the possible damaging resonance of the rhythm of their steps to the natural vibrations of the bridge (a phenomenon that closed the Millennium Bridge in London two days after it first opened).

For Heidegger mood is an attunement between the person and their world, such that mood tunes into certain features of the world, making those aspects 'figural', and in so doing tunes out other aspects, rendering them to the 'ground' and, as such, unnoticed. The analogy of a radio is a good one: as the radio tunes into one station, that station becomes figural and 'fills the air', whilst other stations disappear and become part of the ground. Those other stations are still broadcasting but will only be received if the radio is retuned (at which point the first station disappears). In this view it is mood that organises ('tunes') our experiencing of the world; mood is the source of the gestalt that gives meaning and wholeness to perception and experience.

Check out for yourself the idea that mood attunes us to the world in particular ways:

- See if you can bring to mind an occasion when your mood shifted – say from anxious to excited (for example, when getting exam results) – and whether and how this shifted the whole gestalt of your thinking, feeling and behaviour.

What is the significance of this for coaching? Let's consider coachees who are working in organisations, and return to the theme of mood as personal but not just personal. Mood as attunement enables us to understand that coachees in organisations will be attuned to − and by − the mood of the organisation. In other words, their emotional states resonate to the mood of the organisation, though it's very likely that such states are (mis)attributed to the coachee alone. The coachee may be confused, directionless, lacking confidence, angry and anxious, or be excited, optimistic and enthusiastic. Up to now, and working from our basic model of self- and relationship management, such emotional states have been viewed as primarily about the individual − about their history and how this is manifest in current situations.

This analysis of mood adds a new dimension to our understanding: the coachee's confusion, anxiety and excitement are likely to *also* be a resonance with the confusion, anxiety and excitement of the organisation, and it is vital that this possibility is explored both to deepen understanding of the coachee's situation and the organisation, but also because if it is not then there is the danger that the difficulties of the organisation are personalised and individualised as simply the failings and weaknesses of the coachee. The notion of 'identified patient' in family therapy is relevant here, where the difficulties of the family as a system or field are attributed to one family member who is exhibiting symptoms of unacceptable behaviour or mental illness (Satir 1993). There is an example of this in Chapter 7, in the account of Susan and Alan, where Alan's forthrightness is as much a problem with the culture of the organisation (which mostly avoids conflict) as it is to do with Alan's personality.

It's hard to overstate the importance of this, if for no other reason than coachees are often referred to coaching because they have, or are, a 'problem'. Without the awareness of the likelihood that the coachee is a 'carrier' of the organisational field dynamics, we can do a great disservice to our coachees and compound injustice that may be taking place, probably with all concerned being unaware.

There is another aspect to pick up in the coaching. Our analysis of mood indicates that attunement is a two-way process: the organisation 'tunes' the individual, but what about the other way? How is the individual attuned to the organisation? One way of understanding this is to think of a person's history as a process of being 'tuned' by the family/cultural field in which they grow up, such that the person is sensitised to particular 'wavelengths', like a radio with pre-set buttons for particular stations. They may, for example, be 'sensitive' to criticism, to injustice, to being controlled, and react strongly to these (where maybe, like the Millennium Bridge, resonance with particular 'wavelengths' has dramatic effects).

Other people, who are not so attuned, may not have the same experience, and deny the reality of such things and say it is just the other person's problem: those with a more psychological background are likely to describe this in terms of 'projection'. When a person's 'buttons have been pressed', like the buttons on a radio, something real has been tuned into, something that exists though others may not be so attuned. I have learned through sitting in many groups and in many situations that there is nearly always at least a 'grain of truth' in what others say even if at first I cannot see it (and would maybe prefer not to see it), and for many people that grain can be highly emotionally charged. For example, a team may speak about the high levels of trust present, when one person, in an agitated way, says that he doesn't agree and that it's not safe in the group. Though others initially strongly challenge this view, exploring matters at a deeper level reveals something that is present in the field but only as part of the ground and therefore mostly unnoticed – the shared concerns about confidentiality in the group.

When coaching, therefore, we need to address both aspects of the reciprocal relation between coachee and the field, and in this instance how the coachee has historically been attuned and their resonance to the people and situation they are in; in common parlance, their own contribution to the situation.

There is one vital point I'd like to reiterate. I indicated earlier that mood is the source of a particular view and understanding of the world, which offers both possibilities and limitations for understanding and action. One way of putting this is that mood frames the future. I'm anticipating that you experienced something like this in the earlier mood attunement exercise: when I am anxious or pessimistic I am in a different world to when I'm optimistic and excited. Shifting the mood reveals new possibilities; retuning the station opens up new worlds. It could be said, perhaps with some exaggeration, that the primary task of coaching is to shift moods – of individuals, teams and organisations. How do we do this?

The good news (again) is that we change moods by doing the kind of things we've been discussing throughout the book. We have a deeper understanding now of the importance of mood and emotion, and why it is important to pay close attention to it in the ways we've already described. The most powerful way to shift mood is to first of all stay with the current mood and raise awareness in the ways we've described – through deep listening, empathy and attending to the here and now. Staying with the mood may not be easy because it can evoke its own 'closed world', a field that is emotionally charged and resistant to seeing the world in a different way. Nevertheless, if we can stay with it the existing mood may become more nuanced, with often a complex tapestry of feelings emerging, each of which is a possible opening to the development of a new mood. Through use of self I may notice a sense of hope (which I realise is present but not yet figural for the coachee), share my experience and invite curiosity about this different mood.

There is one more powerful factor in all this: the coaching relationship itself, which is a new element in the field of coachee and organisation. It is quite likely that you have already experienced for yourself the emotional climate that can develop in coaching: maybe a sense of optimism and hope, maybe a determination to do something differently. The mood we establish with our coachees can be a wellspring that opens new possibilities for the coachee and helps sustain them in a mood that enables these new possibilities to be tried out in the organisation. Let's now consider what this looks like in practice.

I'm coaching Kathryn, who is in her early 30s, white, and (my initial guess) from a working-class background. She is a manager in the housing department of a local authority. She has sought coaching for herself because of the stress she is experiencing at work and the impact of this on her performance in her job and home life. In the first meeting she describes the situation at work, where for as long as she can remember there have been cuts to funding and reorganising of services. The mood in the room is one of despondency and hopelessness. I invite her to pay attention to how she feels right now, and this brings out more of the story. Though she has been good at her job Kathryn now feels inadequate and believes she is failing the tenants who rightly look to her for a good service. As this is the first session I also invite her to tell me a bit more about herself and how she came to take on her current post. She recalls growing up in poor housing in a family struggling financially, and how she was the one who held things together in the family, particularly through a period when her parents split up and eventually divorced. She has a passion for her job which she realises has its roots in her own upbringing.

Interested in the 'not just personal' side of her mood I ask her about what things are like at work, and it quickly becomes obvious that her mood is shared by others. Moreover, as we explore further it becomes clear that the shared feeling is rooted in the reality of trying to manage a service that is constantly subject to cuts, reorganisations, regular 'churn' in personnel, and residents who themselves are struggling to cope with unemployment, changes to benefits, and anxiety about paying rent. Through this discussion Kathryn comes to see that her mood has a reality base: it is part of a wider field that is not just about her; it's also about the real shared circumstances of the staff and recipients of the service she is trying to manage.

The conversation shifts back to the more 'personal' side of the mood – about how she has been 'tuned' by her upbringing, particularly her sense of responsibility for others. She always feels, in every situation (for example, a night out with friends), that somehow it is down to her to hold things together to make things 'right'. She has a deep 'existential' sense of failure, which is a fault line in her sense of self that goes back to when she was small and unable to hold her family together when her parents divorced. At a visceral level, in a way she cannot shake, she feels responsible and guilty for what happened. This is a tearful feelingful conversation, where a whole range of emotions – from anger to laughter – are shared, as she recognises that the same childhood mood is present in her feelings about work.

Kathryn's view of herself and the situation at work have changed in the conversation; she can now see the intersection of her personal history and the reality of work, and how these are woven together in the mood of hopelessness and despondency that pervades her world. But she doesn't know what to do about it. Listening to her I'd been paying attention to the shifts in her mood as she speaks. One thing that struck a chord in me was her mood that briefly arrived 'on the scene' as she spoke about her passion for her work and particularly the service to the residents; here the mood was one of commitment and purpose. I share my sense of the shift in her mood and ask what matters most to her in the work. Without hesitation and in a heartfelt way she says 'it's the residents', and with that the positive mood returns and becomes centre stage, a mood of determination that somehow brings clarity of purpose and a sense of opening up new possibilities.

(Continued)

> *(Continued)*
>
> We both know that nothing has changed in the reality that confronts her, but at the same time there is a profound shift in the field. I have been very moved by Kathryn, her story and her situation, and find in myself that same mood: determination and commitment to offer whatever I can to enable her to do the best job she can. There is a mood of shared optimism in the room, which can be 'held' in the coaching relationship, and serve as a resource for Kathryn as she re-engages with the circumstances and moods she'll encounter again back in the workplace.

MOOD AND FIELD IN RELATED WRITING

I've introduced this account of mood and emotion through the existential philosophy of Heidegger and the gestalt notion of field. However, similar themes of mood and the 'personal but not personal' have been addressed by other writers which it will be useful to mention to enable you to deepen your understanding and link up some of the literature in these areas.

Mood and 'primal leadership'

Writers in the field of emotional intelligence, such as Daniel Goleman, have increasingly become interested in mood. Indeed, mood is becoming a focal point, most particularly in the concept of 'primal leadership', where mood is centre stage. For example, 'Managing your mood and the mood of followers is the primal task of leadership' (Goleman et al. 2001, p. 51). Much of this approach is based upon research in neuroscience, which provides a basis for some of the ideas set out in this chapter. For example, our notion of the person as an 'open system' permeated by the shared mood of the group finds its parallel here in the notion of the 'open-loop nature of the limbic system' (Goleman et al. 2013), whereby our emotional states resonate with the moods of those around us. Linking these ideas to leadership, Goleman et al. argue that the mood of the leader has a particularly important impact on the culture of an organisation: 'The leader's mood is quite literally contagious, spreading quickly and inexorably throughout the business' (ibid., p. 44). In this view, certain positive moods are fundamental to business success, and the leader's task is to learn how to manage their moods accordingly.

I'd recommend that you become familiar with the literature on emotional intelligence, as it has become centre stage for coaching in general, and leadership in particular. The reference to neuroscience and its competency-based approach (i.e. a skills-based, teachable capability) has made it very accessible and popular with organisations who are investing in developing the 'emotional intelligence' of their leaders. I'm also fascinated with the way the language of emotional intelligence takes us back to the original formulation of *Stimmung* – the shared connotations of mood and attunement – because the same kind of language and musical metaphor is present throughout the literature of emotional intelligence and leadership (see, for example, McKee et al. (2008).

The systems psychodynamic approach

The systems psychodynamic approach has been a strong tradition in the UK, mostly associated with the Tavistock Institute (Hirschhorn 1990), and covers very similar ground to the notion of field. It is an approach that explores how the processes, procedures, politics and concerns of organisations impact upon individuals who are 'open systems' to the circulating fields of emotion, thinking and behaviour. A classic example of this is Isabel Menzies Lyth ([1970] 1988), whose seminal research into nursing practices in the UK's National Health Service (NHS) introduced the important concept of 'social defences', exploring how the routines and professional practices in nursing (uniforms, a 'professional manner') function as a defence against the possibly overwhelming anxiety and emotions of caring for the sick and dying. This approach demonstrates how vital it is to understand the impact of the organisation on behaviour and the dangers and inadequacy of purely focusing on the individual rather than the culture (as has perhaps happened in recent 'scandals' in the NHS, where 'uncaring staff' are blamed for poor care of patients).

One concept that I've found particularly valuable from this approach when working with coachees is the notion of 'role'. It is our role in the organisation that is the bridge between ourselves and the organisation; and it is our role that gives us our sense of identity there – as manager, lecturer, CFO, and so on.

Important questions arise around role – questions that profoundly affect the person in that role. For example:

- How clearly defined is the role? Very often it is not clearly defined; indeed, different people in the organisation may have differing views of what the role involves.
- How is the role placed in the 'politics' of the organisation? For example, the role of HR with its multiple and potentially conflicting functions around terms and conditions of employment, complaints, training and development.
- How does the person relate to their role? Do they embrace it? Are they ambivalent about it? Do they hate it, seek to reshape it, not understand it or distance themselves from it?

I have constantly found that issues arising from their role impact coachees powerfully, but often these issues are experienced more as 'individual' problems than something arising from the relation between the individual, their role and the organisation. For example, if the role is not clear – which is so often the case – the coachee may have a sense of confusion, anxiety, lack of confidence and poor performance, which they and others attribute to the coachee's inadequacies: that they are just not up to the job. However, when the role is not clear the issue is *systemic*, not individual. Attending to the system, and getting a handle on what belongs where in terms of individual and organisational responsibility, can be a liberating and empowering experience for the coachee.

IMPLICATIONS FOR PRACTICE

I suggest that before you go any further you reread Chapter 4 through the lens of this chapter, bearing the concepts of field, mood and meaning in mind, as this will deepen your understanding of transference, countertransference and use of self.

I recommend you also consider that:

- The coachee's agenda, mood and emotion may be both personal but also situational – an aspect of a shared field – and it can be important to attend to both aspects.
- Mood and emotion may be an important source of 'data' about the situation, and have an understanding that goes deeper than your current thinking.
- Mood can shape the future and what seems possible, so shifting mood can be a powerful intervention.
- The coaching relationship is a shared field, which can be an important source for creating and sustaining a mood that can shift the coachee's system.

RECOMMENDED READING

Parlett (1991) 'Reflections on field theory', *British Gestalt Journal*, and (1997) 'The unified field in practice', *Gestalt Review*, provide a good introduction to field theory.

There are no simple introductions to Heidegger and mood, primarily because his philosophy is so complex. However, if you are willing to dive in and have a go then William Blattner's (2006) *Heidegger's Being and Time: A Reader's Guide* is a good place to start.

If you are interested in Heidegger, mood and Gendlin's focusing approach there is a paper by Gendlin (1978–9) available online: 'Befindlichkeit: Heidegger and the philosophy of psychology', *Review of Existential Psychology and Psychiatry: Heidegger and Psychology*.

There is also a very good and moving book by Robert Storolow (2011), who is one of the founders of 'Intersubjective Psychoanalysis', entitled *World, Affectivity, Trauma: Heidegger and Post-Cartesian Psychoanalysis*, which explores Heidegger's idea through Storolow's own shattering experience of grief and loss.

I've written a paper for *Coaching Today*, the journal of the coaching division of the British Association for Counselling and Psychotherapy, entitled 'Not just personal: the meaning of moods' (2014), which develops some of the ideas in this chapter on Heidegger and mood.

Two good books on the systems psychodynamic approach are O'Neill (2007) *Executive Coaching with Backbone and Heart* and Brunning (ed.) (2006) *Executive Coaching: Systems Psychodynamic Perspective*.

Whittington (2012) *Systemic Coaching and Constellations* describes a powerful and practical way of understanding and working with systems in coaching. Rooted in systemic family therapy, it demonstrates how the 'field' is 'present' in those who are involved with teams and organisations.

I also strongly recommend Oshry (1999) *Leading Systems: Lessons from the Power Lab* for a powerful, experimental/research-based account of the impact of systems on people in organisations.

6

Culture, Difference and Diversity

Custom is our nature. Pascal (1995)

In the chapters so far, difference and diversity have not figured in our discussion. We've talked about the coach and the coachee as individuals whose characteristics are defined mostly by the role they take in the coaching relationship – as coach or coachee. Due to the conventions of the English language, gender has been signalled ('she' or 'he') but not as something particularly significant. Likewise, none of the other characteristics of ourselves and the people we work with – for example age, race, social class, sexuality, (dis)ability, ethnicity and religion (all the ways we are different and diverse) – have shown up as something to which we should pay attention.

It's easy to coach people as if difference and diversity do not matter. It is a familiar refrain that 'I treat everyone as equal', often said with a kind of defiance and perplexity when questions of, say, sexuality or ethnicity are raised. Yet a little self-reflection will surely show that in reality such characteristics do matter and need to be taken into account. For example, in everyday life whether the person I am with is a woman or a man makes a difference, though often more in a background way rather than the focus of attention. However, it is the background that is the context for what is in the foreground, providing shape and meaning in ways that are mostly outside our awareness.

Our job in this chapter is to make that background figural and explore its impact on the coaching relationship. To do this we'll first need to explore the concept of culture as the source of difference and diversity. We'll then discuss personal and professional identity, with its roots in deeply contested social and political processes. A key theme throughout will be the place of the anxiety that is involved when working with someone who may be of a different race, gender, social class or another of the many possible variations (especially when the difference suggests an imbalance of privilege), and how this anxiety is present in the coaching relationship. Having covered this ground we'll be in a position to address how we can work appropriately with difference, diversity and cross-cultural coaching.

CULTURE

Raymond Williams said that 'Culture is one of the two or three most complicated words in the English language' (2014, p. 86). So what do we mean by it here? Culture is the taken-for-granted way we do things, which is so familiar to us that we hardly notice it; it is the ground from which figures emerge. For example, in Western culture, from our earliest years, we learn everyday social practices such as brushing our teeth, getting dressed, going to school, driving a car, getting a bus, celebrating Christmas or Eid and using a mobile phone, which together constitute a 'way of life'. For most of our everyday activities we don't have to think about what we are doing because we are so thoroughly familiar with what's going on and how to get about that we 'just do it'. We could say that our knowing is 'embodied', a tacit practical understanding. So that, for instance, we know the proper distance to stand from people in the lift and how to shift around if other people come in without giving it prior thought. Indeed, if we were deliberately thinking about these things we'd probably become somewhat awkward and clumsy. We become aware of just how much tacit knowing is the basis of everyday activity if we find ourselves in a different culture, where we don't yet 'know the rules', and a whole range of activities suddenly become uncertain. I'm sure you can bring instances of this to mind for yourself – maybe joining a new organisation and not understanding 'how things work round here' and experiencing the uncertainty and anxiety that this can evoke. Sometime later you may notice that you've become familiar with the place, feel more 'at home'; you've learned, mostly not in a deliberate way, enough of the culture to get by without consciously having to think about it.

IDENTITY

Culture is not just the taken-for-granted way we do things; it is also the basis of our sense of identity. If asked to introduce myself I might say I am a coach, supervisor and lecturer, previously a psychotherapist, married, and a parent of three children. If invited to say more, perhaps introducing myself online where who I am is less obvious, I might add that I'm a man, white, British and in my sixties. Depending on the nature of the conversation I could add more: heterosexual, middle class and atheist. I'm describing myself in terms of dimensions of difference and diversity whose source is the culture in which I live, dimensions that are not superficial layers that can be easily shed (I don't believe there is a 'real me' to be found beneath discardable social roles). Rather they *are me*, the very 'ground' of my being, woven into the fabric of my sense of self. From this perspective, 'self' is a field phenomenon.

> Consider your own cultural profile in terms of the dimensions of difference and diversity: gender, nationality, race, religion, ethnicity, age, (dis)ability, class – and any other dimensions that are significant for you (e.g. sexuality, psychiatric diagnosis, occupation):
>
> • Notice for yourself the significance of these for your sense of identity.
> • Bring to mind occasions when particular dimensions have been especially important.

It's also important to notice that these dimensions of difference and diversity, though fundamental to identity, are not fixed or neutral attributes – rather they shift as the field shifts, reshaped by social and political change. For example, same-sex sexual relations were decriminalised in the UK in 1967, and a whole range of legal measures have been introduced affecting lesbian, gay, bisexual and transgender rights since then, including civil partnerships and same-sex marriage. Such changes have a profound impact on the lives and identities of those involved. They are, at the same time, highly contested fields of social and political struggle that are saturated with intense moral and social judgements, of good/bad, better/worse. This is evident again in same-sex relations, where the opponents of such activity denounce it as sinful, and in many countries it is still punishable by imprisonment or the death penalty. The anxiety experienced around difference and diversity is a signal that we are not just dealing with personal matters of unconscious bias or prejudice; we are also engaging with conflicted cultural processes (religious beliefs, laws, vested interests) that are ever-present in our lives.

We are socialised into the many dimensions of identity from the moment of birth; they are woven into the fabric of our being in that same tacit, embodied way as other aspects of the culture we live in. Because of this, and because such relations are fashioned and refashioned in fields of social and political action, we can never fully comprehend them, never get to the bottom of how they shape us. I can seek to raise my awareness of the issues but this awareness can only reach so far, precisely because the source of who I am, though experienced personally, is not just personal but cultural. In a very real sense, who I am is 'beyond me'; if there is an unconscious it is as much (or more) cultural as personal.

I had a sobering example of this 'cultural unconscious' in the naming of our children. I like to think of myself as someone who supports equality between men and women. It was a shock when I found myself insisting to my partner that our children took my surname. I experienced this at a deep, feelingful, visceral level, a hard-wired imperative that I'd never given a second thought to before. The whole history and contemporary political and social dynamics of relations between men and women that is an ever-present part of who I am was present in that conflicted moment – and the children have my surname. Would I change that decision now if I could go back and have that moment again? No. There is still something cultural that viscerally 'has me', woven into me that I cannot get past even though cognitively I can see how my behaviour is shaped by and perpetuates patriarchal relations in our culture. Likewise with the many other dimensions of difference and diversity: they are embedded in our cultural norms and thus embedded in us in ways we can never fully grasp or 'escape from'; they are the very 'ground of our being'. Language is a good example of this – try speaking or writing in English in a non-gendered way.

DIFFERENCE, DIVERSITY AND THE COACHING RELATIONSHIP

What are the implications of our discussion for the coaching relationship? Let's begin with ourselves.

I'd like you to sit with yourself for a few minutes and bring to mind the first time, or a significant time, when you felt different to the people around you. Allow yourself to recall this time:

- Where are you?
- Who is involved?
- What is happening?
- Take time to connect with what you are feeling, thinking and doing in these moments.

The exercise invites consideration of the past, but maybe (and quite likely) these, or other experiences like them, are also current and ongoing. Take a moment to notice if and where you have a sense of difference in your life now.

How were you with the question? When I ask it of myself I don't find occasions that readily spring to mind. Then again, I am white, British, male, able bodied, middle class and heterosexual. There is something important in this: I am on the 'right side' of all these dimensions, the right side of these power gradients, the side that in our culture is socially sanctioned as 'good', which can render the social divisions virtually invisible in my everyday experience. I'm swimming with the tide rather than against it and don't experience the constant pressure, the constant 'splash' of discrimination. These dimensions don't become figural; they remain as the ground.

When I stay with the question a little longer what comes to mind is living in an ethnically diverse inner city and sometimes being in shops where I am the only white person present. Suddenly I notice that there is a sense of 'standing out' which I never experience in predominantly white groups, and I feel a bit awkward and uncertain, not sure what is being said or how I'm regarded by those around me. No one seems to particularly notice me and people are polite when serving me, but somehow this sense of 'difference' pervades the whole situation. I find myself monitoring and wondering about our behaviours towards each other: am I being particularly polite? Are they?

What I get a glimpse of is a constant everyday reality for people who are on the 'wrong side' of these dimensions of difference, for whom it is the differences that are figural. They are likely to be confronted daily by the impact of being different, perhaps with an accompanying range of feelings such as anger, fear, confusion, self-doubt or withdrawal, all of which are often laced with a determination to resist what might be termed 'internalised oppression' and seek to positively assert their own identity.

Let's take this more directly into the coaching relationship with a second question. Imagine you are in a coaching session with:

- a white middle-class woman
- an Afro-Caribbean woman
- a wealthy white man, educated at Eton and Oxford
- a young woman in a wheelchair
- a gay man
- a Muslim woman wearing a burka
- a refugee
- a deaf Asian man
- a white working-class man
- a Catholic priest
- an Imam.

We could endlessly add to this list but first I'd invite you to consider your own cultural profile and how this 'positions' you in our culture. With whom might you feel most at ease or most challenged, and what cultural dynamics are likely to be in play as you meet others with a different cultural profile? With the list above, do some people stand out more than others for you, and if so what does this potentially say about your relations with them? If their identity does not seem particularly significant, perhaps you are meeting a person very much like yourself. This raises a question: to what extent does a shared positioning in the world create and limit the possibilities of our work together? If we share the same 'ground', what 'figures' remain invisible? Or, again, if their identity doesn't seem significant, perhaps it is because you are on the 'right side' of the power imbalance, unaware that the difference is very significant to the other person.

Let's take this another step. I asked you to imagine you are in a coaching session with these different people and I am guessing you positioned yourself as the coach. If you did I would now like you to go through the exercise again, but this time from the position of coachee. What would it be like to encounter these people if you are the coachee and they are the coach? If from this different perspective their identities are now figural ask yourself why: how has changing roles changed the significance of identities?

Gathering up the strands of our reflections, it's clear that our original conception of the coaching relationship as simply between coach and coachee as individuals in roles was too abstract. We need to revise our basic diagram to catch some of the many dimensions of difference that are ever-present in the field, but are often background rather than foreground. When we bring them to the fore the coaching relationship suddenly seems very crowded – a rich field of cultural diversity.

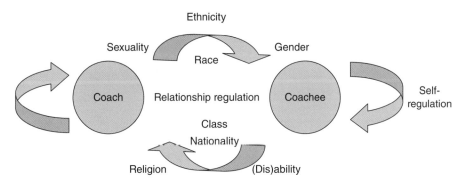

FIGURE 6.1   Cultural diversity and the coaching relationship

DIFFERENCE, DIVERSITY AND ANXIETY

How might difference become figural in the conversation? Well it might be that the coachee brings it into the conversation because it is important to them ('Have you any experience of working with people with disability?') or it is an important aspect of the coaching agenda ('I think I didn't get the job because I'm a woman'). I believe that something else often happens when diversity becomes figural: an **anxiety** that saturates the relationship and complicates all we do. Some of these dynamics are identified in Figure 6.2.

Difference and diversity invisible. This may be because particular dimensions of difference and diversity are present but not apparent, for example sexuality or a medical/psychiatric diagnosis such as depression. Alternatively, they may be 'visible' but do not 'matter', and this 'not mattering' renders the difference virtually invisible. For example, as a man I may notice gender differences but consider that they don't matter ('I treat everyone the same') and this move makes gender seemingly insignificant. There will be little or no awareness of difference in this position, and with that, little or no anxiety.

Difference and diversity avoided. Here difference is figural, and with this noticing comes anxiety that makes it hard to address. Again, drawing upon my own identity it may be that my coachee is black, or deaf, or gay, and maybe

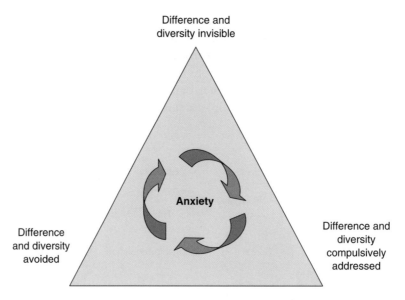

Difference and
diversity invisible

Anxiety

Difference
and diversity
avoided

Difference and
diversity
compulsively
addressed

FIGURE 6.2

this difference is important for the coaching agenda, but I cannot bring myself to speak about it for fear of offending, of saying or doing the wrong thing – anxious perhaps, at a deeper level, of tapping into the 'ground' of social/political dynamics of privilege, discrimination and oppression in which, in some sense, I am 'guilty'/complicit.

Difference and diversity compulsively addressed. Here difference and diversity is entangled with 'should' and 'must' that often have their origin in professional training, which in turn is often driven by the anxiety of organisations and professions seeking to demonstrate that they are doing the right thing around difference and diversity. It may also be written into policies and procedures detailing required behaviours. As a practitioner I ***must*** address the differences. This does not take away the anxiety; indeed it may well compound it as there is the additional twist that I feel compelled to do what I am so anxious about. There is a likelihood that this sense of compulsion will result in clumsy ill-timed interventions which can reinforce the anxiety in the relationship.

The arrows in Figure 6.2 indicate that the points of the triangle are not fixed positions, but poles between which we may circle depending upon the situation and people involved. A dimension of difference may be more or less visible; the tension between avoidance and compulsively addressing something may change as the relationship develops. Also, there may be some dimensions of difference and diversity with which I am more comfortable than others, and therefore less driven by anxiety in how I respond.

> Consider your own behaviour in terms of the diagram:
>
> - Are there dimensions of difference you feel comfortable with, such that you would be ready to engage with them when it's appropriate to do so?
> - Are there dimensions of difference that are invisible to you, though maybe other people are saying you are missing something important?
> - Are there relationships where you know that difference is important but you are not addressing it?
> - Do you feel a compulsion in yourself to identify and address difference in certain situations?

WORKING APPROPRIATELY WITH DIFFERENCE AND DIVERSITY

If we are to work appropriately with difference and diversity we have to step out of the triangle and find a way of relating where difference and diversity is visible and spoken about, in a way and at a time that is not driven by rules, 'shoulds', 'musts' and 'oughts'. We are seeking a relationship where difference and diversity are part of the conversation because they have a natural place there and may be important for the coachee and their coaching agenda.

To have this kind of conversation we'll have to address the anxiety that is almost bound to arise, and recognise that the relationship is unlikely to ever be anxiety-free, as the underlying political and social dynamics of difference that generate the underlying sense of anxiety will always be present. So 'anxiety-lite' rather than anxiety-free might be a better way to describe the likely optimal state of the relationship, and recognising the presence of this anxiety may be a good signal and guide that there is something important to address.

How do we establish such a relationship? Talking to people I've seen who do this, and drawing on my own experience when things have gone well, the way forward seems very 'simple', but like many simple things not necessarily easy to do. So before I proceed I'd like you to consider for yourself what's involved.

> - What do you see as the way forward in establishing the kind of relationship that enables the conversation about difference and diversity?
> - What have you noticed about people who seem able to enter into such conversations?
> - What has enabled you to have such conversations?

My understanding is that such conversations happen when there is:

- Real trust, respect and connection.
- Safety to talk about things that may be very painful and full of feeling.

- Mutual care, concern and liking of each other.
- An openness to learn from one another.
- A sense of joint exploration.
- An understanding that each other's positive intentions make the issues figural.

How does this line up with your thoughts and reflections? You'll see that it's all about the quality of the relationship – simple in one sense, but not easy to achieve. The good news is that the kind of approach to coaching we've been developing has the possibility of enabling the kind of conversation we've outlined:

- We've seen the importance of contracting to establish proper boundaries and confidentiality and safety.
- The whole coaching approach is about raising awareness in a way that respects the coachee's own pace and readiness to share.
- Identifying and working with the coachee's agenda provides a context and frame for judgements as to when and how to address issues.
- Use of self provides a way of working that enables the coach to notice what is happening and sharing what's 'in the field' in a way that is attuned to the developing relationship.
- Drawing together all of the above, it is likely that such an approach enables a genuine meeting, liking and respect between coach and coachee, where a sense of common shared humanity invites a deeper exploration of difference and diversity, which can be enriching to both parties.

So if we are not to rely on rules to guide us, how are we to know when to include difference and diversity in the conversation? The answer is related to the fact that opening up the subject in the first place can seem like the hardest thing to do. People develop their own style around this and it comes down to personal and professional judgement about the relationship and when and how to address difference:

- It might be that I meet a coachee who is blind, or in a wheelchair, and notice I feel a bit awkward because I don't know if they need something from me to navigate the place where we meet. If this happens it's likely I'll ask what they'd like from me. This, in turn, may lead in to more of a conversation about how we are together and the possibility of discussing the significance of blindness or wheelchair use in relation to the coaching agenda.
- It might be that in our initial 'getting to know each other' conversation we discover something about our similarities and differences which on the one hand can deepen our relationship, and on the other hand can be a reference point in subsequent conversations of the coachee's agenda. It might be, for example, that my coachee has a strong religious faith which I don't have, and this is significant in how we understand and deal with issues.

- It might be that a difference between us which is obvious, such as gender, has not been spoken about, but I find myself wondering about it as the coachee tells her story and I take the initiative to raise it. For example, my coachee may be working in a very male-dominated senior team, and I may enquire about gender as a factor in the situation even though she has not yet mentioned it, as I'm guessing it is important here. As part of the conversation this might be an opportunity to talk about us; about whether and what part gender plays in our relationship.

You'll notice that in each of these examples there are two aspects to attend to: how we are as coach and coachee in the coaching relationship, and the relevance of difference to the coaching agenda.

Overall I think the approach is to be 'difference and diversity aware', so as to address it at a time and in a way that is woven into the developing relationship and flow of the conversation. Anxiety will be often present and sometimes I may 'get it wrong' – saying something that is not quite right, using language that is not 'correct', offering assistance that's not needed, making assumptions that are mis placed and so forth. It is important to understand at this point that the anxiety is likely to be mostly *my anxiety* and not the coachee's, who may be very familiar with the tangles people get themselves into seeking to say and do the right thing. The 'anxiety-lite' way forward is to be bold enough to speak through the anxiety, and open enough to hear back from the coachee regarding what they've made of what I've said and done. If I've misattuned, and they feel safe enough to tell me, then we can take it from there.

What might this look like in practice?

My coachee Tom is a middle manager in a large retail organisation, where he has worked for 15 years, starting off on the 'shop floor' and gradually working his way up to more senior posts. The organisation recognises that he has talent and wants to support him through coaching to realise his potential, with the possibility of him becoming a member of the senior leadership team. The challenge for Tom, which he recognises, is his relationships with those in authority; whilst he is excellent at dealing with those lower down the organisation he always finds himself clashing with other managers and those in more senior positions. He knows that if he does not address this then he will not progress further in the organisation.

I invite Tom to tell me about himself and what he understands about his relationships with others. He begins by telling me about his background: growing up in a poor working-class environment, leaving school with few qualifications, and how he has since climbed his way up the ladder in the organisation. He has some understanding of the behaviour he displays at work towards colleagues. He feels very rooted in his working-class origins, with a pervasive sense of 'them and us' that enables

(Continued)

(Continued)

him to naturally ally with those on the shop floor, whereas he feels different from colleagues in managerial and senior positions, the very group he now belongs to and, in some sense, aspires to. He particularly struggles with those who have joined the organisation through graduate schemes and are now senior to him. He recognises in himself a potentially explosive cocktail of feelings: lack of confidence, shame about being 'not good enough', and anger (almost rage, contempt or loathing) for those from privileged backgrounds who get jobs through fancy education and connections. The depth of the challenge he faces becomes very apparent to both of us as he recounts his story.

As we meet and talk I am aware of a lot happening for me. I am uncomfortable to recognise that Tom's working-class origins were apparent to me from the moment we met; from the way he spoke, his accent, something about the manner in which he dressed and moved, and in the background a doubt in me as to whether he had the capability for senior leadership. Unconscious bias arose from the moment we met – and of course he will meet this bias in many of his colleagues. Something else is present too: my own history. My family was structured around class divisions. My mother was a very working-class Londoner, proud of her origins and scathing about anyone who put on 'airs and graces'. My father was middle class and university educated. I left school with few qualifications but my career has taken me in a middle-class direction, including university, but I can easily feel different and 'unmannered' with 'posh' people and in 'posh' settings. I know my use of language and accent can shift depending on the people I'm with, so I get a sense of straddling class divides, and I become aware with Tom of a more working-class lilt in my voice. I also have an intimation that somewhere in me is my mother's distain for those who 'get above their station' which has cast a shadow over how I've lived my life and might, unless I am very mindful of it, cast a shadow over my work with Tom.

I'm sure you can see the struggle for Tom that has to be addressed in the coaching as he, in a sense, seeks to join 'them'. You'll also get a feel for the complexity of my own history, as the coach, in relation to Tom: how that history can be a source of empathy and yet at the same time, in its own way, cast a shadow that limits the possibilities of our work together. Alongside this are the biases and prejudices that permeate our beings, through membership of a culture where there are still powerful class divisions. It goes without saying that supervision is going to be vital in this work, with the constant priority of attending to my own personal cultural/historical involvement in the coaching relationship.

CROSS-CULTURAL COACHING

Difference and diversity refers primarily to the relationships we encounter **within** a particular culture of a recognisably distinct entity such as a country like the UK. Cross-cultural refers to relationships **between** cultures that are recognisably distinct: for example, between the cultures of the UK and Singapore. Of course, we also recognise that such distinctions can be varied and nuanced – we talk about a mining or fishing community, or the culture of a family or an organisation. These are cultures that sit within a wider shared community. Likewise there are communities that have, through immigration, become part of a wider community whilst retaining much of their own identity, such as Pakistani or Polish communities in the UK.

Each of these communities will have their own positions on issues of difference and diversity (for example, on gender), and at the same time there are complex and challenging relationships between the cultures as each accommodates, assimilates, creatively combines and sometimes rejects the values and behaviours of other groups. The greatest challenge can be for people who have a foot in more than one culture, who can live in both but may not belong properly to either. In a sense Tom was living between cultures, between 'them' and 'us' but belonging to neither, and this was a source of great confusion, disorientation and strong feeling (for example, of being disloyal to 'us').

Let's focus on the cross-cultural, as that realm where cultures are distinct, to explore what challenges and possibilities this poses for coaching. If we return to our original discussion of culture you'll recall that I spoke of it as the taken-for-granted way we do things, which is so familiar to us that we hardly notice it. We have a tacit, embodied sense of how things are and what we should do, so much of the time we act out of habit, without forethought, because we 'know our way around'. It is precisely this tacit, embodied sense that becomes the 'problem' when working across cultures, as the taken-for-granted understanding and ways of doing things are likely to lead us astray.

For example, I casually accept a business card that has been carefully and respectfully handed to me by my guest from Singapore, putting it into my pocket with hardly a glance, unaware that in doing so I am likely to have offended him. I reach out to shake the hand of a women whose cultural background forbids public physical contact with men. I begin to walk into the house of a colleague where people take their shoes off at the entrance. In each case, in doing what I normally do I make the wrong move and, like not noticing a step on the path, the shock can be sudden and intense. I'm likely to experience a surge of embarrassment, perhaps shame, at violating the expectations of 'what one does' in such situations. How do we proceed in such circumstances, where there is the background anxiety of unwittingly making the wrong move?

My taken-for-granted way of doing things can lead me astray but the issue runs deeper still. It is likely that fundamental assumptions I make about people and the nature of the world we live in, which shape my thinking and feeling, are specific to my culture but I take them as universal; that is, I take them to apply to everyone. I encountered this very directly many years ago working as a therapist in an inner city in the UK. My frame of reference was the individual and notions of personal responsibility and self-actualisation (not dissimilar, as I'm sure you can see, to the fundamental assumptions of coaching). Such a frame of reference left me ill-equipped and wrong-footed when I worked with a Pakistani client, where for her the family rather than the individual was primary, and notions of honour and duty more important than self-actualisation and individual choice. So in working across cultures I have to be ready to encounter very different ways of construing the fundamental 'categories' of existence and human relationships.

This challenge of coaching across cultures has grown as more and more coaches work with individuals and teams in multinational and global corporations, so for many people this is familiar territory. How then do we reach out and address the kind of issues we've identified that have the potential to derail the coaching relationship? One approach has been the development of what has been called 'cultural intelligence' (Peterson 2004; Livermore 2010), defined by Peterson as:

> the ability to engage in a set of behaviours that use skills (i.e. language or interpersonal skills) and qualities (e.g. tolerance for ambiguity, flexibility) that are attuned to the culture-based values and attributes of the people with whom one interacts. (2004, p. 89)

A favourite element of such an approach is to identify what the authors see as the key dimensions of culture, and to invite the reader to organise their understanding of different cultures along these dimensions (e.g. Passmore 2013; Rosinski 2003; Peterson 2004; Trompenaars and Hampden-Turner 2012). For example, Trompenaars and Hampden-Turner have five key dimensions: universalism versus particularism, individualism versus communitarianism, neutral versus affective, specific versus diffuse, and achievement versus ascription. Peterson also has five scales: equality versus hierarchy, direct versus indirect, individual versus group orientation, task versus relationship, and risk versus caution.

My struggle with a client who focused on the family rather than the individual is an example of the individualism versus communitarian dimension, and gave me a sense of how fundamental these assumptions are, and how disorienting it can be when working with someone whose world view has such different roots.

The meaning and significance of some of these dimensions of culture may not be immediately clear; rather than give detailed explanations I invite you to explore them for yourself in the various texts. Then again, it might be that you are, have been or know of cultures that have different dimensions of culture: do any come to mind for you?

Such literature is a way into cross-cultural coaching and a useful source of knowledge about working with other cultures. Perhaps more fundamental, however, is a desire to reach out and 'meet' the other person, as underlying all the many differences there is a shared common humanity. In this sense working cross-culturally is no different to our usual practice, where the deepest challenge is always to connect with the other person. The recognition and management of anxiety is again a key issue, in this case the anxiety that comes from uncertainties of not being culturally attuned and making 'mistakes' in the relationship. The obvious cultural differences present an opportunity here: of recognising from the beginning the inevitability of difference and agreeing to check in with each other; explicitly noticing and addressing difference and getting to know and appreciate each other. This might be described as the 'open-hearted approach', with the potential to be fulfilling for all parties.

IMPLICATIONS FOR PRACTICE

What are the implications of this chapter for your practice?

- What is your 'cultural profile' in terms of the dimensions of difference and diversity?
- What do you think is the significance of your profile in the co-creation of the coaching relationship?
- Are there dimensions of difference and diversity that are very apparent to you? Are there some that hardly figure?
- Are you addressing the difference and diversity in the coaching relationship? Bring to mind the coachees you are working with and notice if, when and how you are doing this.

RECOMMENDED READING

Passmore (2013) *Diversity in Coaching: Working with Gender, Culture, Race and Age* provides a good overview of the subject and is a resource for considering coaching with coachees from a range of different cultural backgrounds and dimensions of difference.

Rosinski (2003) *Coaching Across Cultures*, Peterson (2004) *Cultural Intelligence* and Trompenaars and Hampden-Turner (2012) *Riding the Waves of Culture* provide frameworks for working cross-culturally.

Frost (2014) *The Inclusion Imperative* is highly recommended. It tells the story of inclusion and the London Olympic Games of 2012. Reading this inspiring book I really came to understand the concrete meaning of the statement that 'Diversity is not the problem; it's the solution'. Such a shift in perspective opens up often unexplored territory and possibilities for our coachees and for ourselves.

7

Coaching in Organisations: Managing Complex Relationships

So far we've explored the coaching relationship primarily from the perspective of working with coachees on a pro bono basis. Though organisations have been present, they've been in the background as a context within which the coaching takes place, without impacting on the coaching relationship itself. This way of viewing the set-up is reminiscent of the classic therapy relationship, where there is a therapist and coachee bounded by a confidentiality contract that sets them apart from the rest of the world. Most coaching, however, takes place within a context where the organisation is very present and has a significant impact on the coaching relationship. In this chapter we'll bring the organisation more into focus and make it figural rather than the ground, a shift in perspective that is invited, in large part, by the move you'll make upon the completion of your first coaching programme, as you take the L-plates off and your identity changes from a coach-in-training to a qualified coach.

Why have I linked graduating from your coaching programme with the shift in the significance of the organisation? Primarily because you and the organisation enter into a relationship in a different way; you become important to each other and have to take each other into account. Representing this in its most simple form, there is a shift from a two-party to a three-party, triangular relationship, a shift that has a profound impact upon the coaching relationship (Figure 7.1).

There are two major kinds of relationship between the coach and the organisation: (1) the coach who is external and (2) the coach who is internal to the organisation. We shall explore both in this chapter.

If you are setting out as an independent coach you'll want to begin charging a fee, and will encounter the challenge of how to market yourself. It's likely you'll have to 'sell yourself' as a coach, and many people find this extremely difficult.

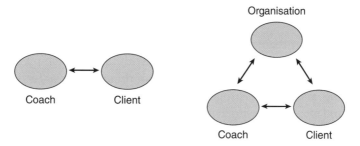

FIGURE 7.1   From two-party to three-party relationships

Am I good enough? Will I be 'found out'? Will I be able to deliver the goods? Can I make a living out of this? This is fertile ground for the 'imposter syndrome', the sense of taking on an identity which you may not yet truly own. You'll see that already something new has entered the coaching relationship – the 'commercial' element and all this involves in terms of your sense of identity as a coach, both in the coaching relationship itself and in your relations with the organisation.

If your intention is to become an internal coach then you too will experience a shift as you graduate from the programme. It's likely you'll take on the identity of a coach within the organisation, someone who is seen as knowing about coaching even though you may still feel you are finding your way rather than having arrived as a coach. You'll probably join the coaching service offered by the organisation and encounter the impact of the way that service is organised and offered to employees. It's likely the coaching you do will be in addition to your 'day job', and you'll encounter the extraordinary complexity that comes from coaching people within the same organisation in which you work.

I've been painting a picture of my sense of what it's like as you move towards the conclusion of your first coaching programme and make the transition from coach-in-training to qualified coach.

Take a few minutes to consider how this connects with your experience – as anticipated, current, or recalled – and how you view the significance of the organisation in this transition.

Let's have a look at some of the key issues that arise when coaching in organisations. These include:

1. Who is the client?
2. Overlapping relationships.
3. Dual roles.

1. WHO IS THE CLIENT?

This may seem rather a strange question because the answer is so obvious – surely the client is the person you work with in the coaching sessions? And everything we've said so far sets up that view of things, as we've focused on pro bono coaching and haven't properly considered the organisation. Yet as you become an independent or internal coach where an organisation is paying a fee for your services there is a strong case for saying that the organisation is the client; you are providing a service which they are paying for. So who is the client: the person you meet in the coaching room or the organisation that is paying you to do the coaching? And to push the question one step further, whose agenda are we working on? Again, is it the agenda of the person you meet in the room or the agenda of the organisation paying for your service?

These are very tricky, fundamental questions that go to the heart of coaching in organisations. So who is the coachee and whose agenda are you working on?

Take some time to consider your view here because how you answer will profoundly shape how you go about your coaching and the whole nature of the coaching relationship.

I am anticipating that, having set up this conundrum, you are now expecting a neat answer. Unfortunately I don't have one, partly because it is possible to take up different positions with good arguments in support of each. At one end of the spectrum there are coaches who are adamant that the person they meet in the coaching room is the client – after all, the approach to coaching we've been describing is founded upon the belief in the capacity of the client to make sense of and act upon their situation. On the other hand there are coaches who are clear that the organisation is the client with a right to shape the agenda because they are commissioning the work and looking for a return on their investment. So I don't think a definitive answer is attainable, but what we can do is get as clear as we can about what is involved and then find out what 'sits right' for each of us as a coach: that is, a position which you can justify to yourself and others, which gives guidance as to how to go about your practice.

There is another reason why, in practice rather than in principle, it is hard to come up with a definitive answer. The word 'organisation' has been used as if it refers to a distinct definable entity which will always have a clear view on things. The reality is very different, a reality perhaps better described as 'messy' because what we encounter in organisations is a variety of people who are likely to understand the purpose of coaching differently, and have different motivations for being involved. Let's give some examples of what you may encounter.

You might be invited to coach where:

1. A valued employee is having a difficult time, and could do with some extra support and development, though those commissioning the coaching don't have a clear idea about coaching and the process involved.
2. A manager takes the view that the coaching agenda is between the coach and coachee and therefore does not expect any involvement in the work.
3. There are a number of people involved in the commissioning of the coaching who have different ideas about the place and purpose of coaching. For example, HR may want a say on who receives coaching and the kind of agenda that is appropriate, perhaps as part of a wider organisational policy, whilst a line manager (perhaps being unclear about the organisational policy on coaching) has a differing view, and initiates coaching for a direct report on that basis.
4. Agreement has been reached (or not) between all parties, and then one of the parties leaves and is replaced by a new person who has a different view of the appropriateness of coaching and the agenda. For example, a new line manager may say that it is performance management rather than coaching that is needed. In such situations (which are quite frequent), part way through the coaching the whole thing may need to be recontracted, or maybe the coaching continues amidst a background sense of uncertainty and confusion.
5. Coaching is offered as part of a talent management programme and all those on the programme have their own coach for, say, four sessions, with an agenda that arises out of their participation on the programme. The person being coached, and going along with the programme requirements, turns up to the first session with no clear idea about coaching, its place in the programme, and what to expect, and conveys a sense of 'OK, well I'm here, coach me then'.
6. The organisation has a well-formed policy on coaching: they are very selective on whom they take on as coaches in terms of qualifications, accreditation and experience; and are very clear about the coaching agenda, how it is going to be evaluated, and the kind of feedback that needs to be sent back to the organisation from the sessions.

I am sure you can see that in these cases (and there are many variations on these themes) how coaching is positioned in the organisation, the understanding and expectations of those involved, and the frequent 'churn' in personnel can indeed be described as 'messy'. How do you manage all of this? How can you navigate a course that keeps intact the integrity of the coaching process? We'll see that these questions arise repeatedly when working in organisations, but how can you address this messiness in relation to the particular question under consideration here? Who is the client and whose agenda is it?

One simple strategy is: get clear about terminology. Up to now in this chapter we've allowed the word 'client' to cover both the person being coached and the organisation commissioning the work. Let's retain the word 'coachee' for the person being coached, and 'sponsor' for the person(s) in the organisation who have a direct interest in setting up and signing off the coaching. The sponsor may be the line manager or include other people, perhaps someone in HR responsible for organising and buying in coaching in the organisation. So, to rephrase my earlier question, how can we address the inherent messiness in the relations between coach, coachee and sponsor?

The golden rule is *contracting*, and getting the contract as clear as possible with the parties involved. We've already discussed the fundamental significance of contracting, getting the 'frame' right, in one-to-one pro bono coaching, and the same principles apply here – though as we'll see, things get far more complicated. Nevertheless, the same principles apply. We need to create a safe (or safe enough) 'container' for the coaching, which involves secure boundaries as the foundation for the trust required for people to share and explore what's important to them. The difference from pro bono coaching is that now the frame must also include the proper boundaries and relations with the sponsor and other people in the organisation.

The ideal is to get clarity with each of the relevant parties, which is likely to involve:

- Separate one-to-one conversations with each person to check out their understanding of coaching, get their candid view of the situation, and agree the purpose of the proposed coaching.
- The parties involved meeting together in the same room (or it might be on the phone or video conferencing) and having an honest conversation to agree the purpose and goal(s) of the coaching.
- Addressing key issues such as confidentiality, additional data collection (e.g. 360-degree feedback) and how the coaching will be evaluated.

Sometimes the contracting will be a positive and straightforward process, but there will be other times when it is somewhat messy. For example, you'll encounter times when participants are not always entirely honest in these one-to-one and three-way meetings, perhaps holding back on things they might say about one another and what they see as the purpose of coaching. It might be that the line manager is frustrated with their direct report and sees coaching as a last resort, perhaps to demonstrate that they've done all they can, before exiting the person from the organisation. On the other side, it might be that the person to be coached is going along with the process because they see it as politic to do so, and it emerges in the next coaching session that they have an entirely different view of the agenda or even whether they want coaching at all. These examples are some worse-case scenarios, though not that unusual. In the middle are all the variations on what is and what is not being said, issues of trust between parties, and conflicting views of the purpose of coaching. It can also be quite an achievement to set up such a meeting in the first place. For a host of reasons, such as difficulty with diaries, cancellation of agreed dates, or apparent but hard-to-pin-down reluctance to meet by one or more parties, the coaching may be well under way or practically over without such a meeting taking place. Let's have a look at an example to make this a bit more concrete.

John has just completed his diploma in coaching and receives a call from Susan, a senior manager in a public sector organisation in which John had previously worked. She is interested in the possibility of John doing some coaching with one of her direct report. They meet, and she tells John she would like him to coach Alan, who has been outstanding at getting results, but some of his behaviours are a cause for concern. She very much wants to keep Alan in the organisation as she can see his talent and potential to move into a more senior leadership role, but his lack of awareness and tact when dealing with colleagues across the organisation is damaging and putting his future in jeopardy. John asks her whether she has spoken to Alan about the situation and the reason for the coaching. It becomes clear that Susan has held back from saying to Alan about how she views him, both his potential and the negative impact he is having. She finds having that kind of candid conversation hard to do. They agree that John will meet with Alan for an initial 'chemistry' meeting, followed by a three-way meeting between them all.

John and Alan meet to discuss the possibility of coaching and what the agenda would be. Alan is a bit cynical about the whole thing. He has come into the post from a very performance-focused private sector background and is rather dismissive of what he regards as the pussyfooting behaviour of others, including Susan. He sees the problem as more with them than him, though he can see that it wouldn't go down well if he simply refused the coaching. John acknowledges Alan's view and asks him whether there is a way he could frame the coaching agenda so there would be real benefit for him and he could engage rather than just going along with it for appearances, something John is not prepared to collude with. Alan agrees that there needs to be a real purpose for them to meet and that he will give it some thought, ready for the three-way meeting with Susan.

At this meeting John invites Susan and Alan to share their views of the purpose and agenda for the coaching. He has spoken to both of them so knows some of their 'back story' and wonders how honest they'll be with each other. Susan says how much the organisation values Alan and can see his potential to progress to more senior positions, but she somewhat waters down her concerns about his behaviour and its likely impact on his future in the organisation. She couches the purpose and agenda of coaching in terms of helping him settle in more with his relatively new role. Alan is much more straightforward in giving his views, and voices his doubts that there is a genuine issue to address and about the value of coaching.

John begins to realise that the problem lies as much with Susan as with Alan, though he feels somewhat stuck as he does not have permission to disclose what Susan said in their initial meeting. In light of Alan's doubts that there is a real issue to address in coaching, John invites Susan to say more about her reasons for suggesting coaching, and she summons up the courage to be more blunt about Alan's impact on others and the implications of this for his future. Susan's candour shifts the picture somewhat for Alan and an agenda is agreed whereby Alan will explore how he can be more effective within

(Continued)

(Continued)

the different culture in which he now works; not to water down his focus on performance but how he communicates with colleagues in a way that does not cause damage and get their backs up. If he can be successful in communicating better then both he and the organisation will 'win'.

They also agree at this meeting that John will have informal conversations with key people about their experience of working with Alan, and how he could develop his communication with them, and that he'll give feedback on any emerging themes in the coaching sessions. Confidentiality is agreed, as is: what success would look like, lines of communication between John, Susan and Alan, how many sessions and when a review will take place. There is a sense at the end of the meeting of a much greater shared understanding and purpose – the sense of a proper coaching 'frame' for the work which all three parties can sign up to.

So what is there to learn from this example?

First, taking an even-handed approach to the sponsor and coachee is important. You can also help the sponsor get clear about the purpose of the coaching. For example, you might ask variations on the themes of:

- 'What is your understanding of coaching?'
- 'What are your goals for the coaching, and what would success look like?'
- 'From what you know of the coachee's situation, what might help or hinder the work?'
- 'Who are the other important stakeholders and what are the issues to be aware of?'
- 'What is your relationship like with the coachee, and how might that impact the coaching?'

Likewise with the coachee:

- 'What is your understanding of coaching?'
- 'Do you want coaching?'
- 'What do you see as the coaching agenda and what would success look like?'
- 'What do you see as the main challenges and opportunities here?'
- 'Do you have any concerns about us working together?'

Second, the coach can do important work not just in the one-to-one sessions but also by facilitating communication between the interested parties, particularly in the three-way meeting (in a way similar to 'couple coaching'), as the issues are often as much about their relationships as it is about the coaching agenda. Indeed, as again is evident in this example, it may be that the coach is being invited, in effect, to deliver a message or address issues that properly belong to others in the organisation, in this instance the line manager. Careful contracting in which each party speaks honestly about the purpose and agenda of the coaching can lessen the chances that the coaching is set up as 'management by proxy', in which the coach is invited to tackle problems others are avoiding.

A further point to consider is that the 'messiness' may well present important 'data' about the organisation and how it functions. In our example, the pussyfooting identified by Alan as a feature of the organisation has emerged in Susan's inability to be honest with Alan. Indeed, the whole coaching agenda that Susan proposed may resonate with something about the organisational culture, where people hold back from speaking directly to each other, a culture where Alan's manner is out of place. It is important, therefore, to take note of the process you are involved in, notice its impact on you and others, and consider what it says about the culture of the organisation.

Transactional analysis places a lot of emphasis on contracting and has useful models (Lapworth and Sills 2011; Sills 2012), which I've adapted in Figure 7.2, that aid thinking about three-party contracting. It enables us to consider the relative attention and the 'distance' we are paying to each party in the relationship.

In (a) there is equal distance between all parties; the coach is paying attention to the practical and psychological distance between herself, the coachee and the sponsor. This is the set-up to aim for, where each party can take up their proper role and responsibilities in the coaching. This is the situation we arrived at with Susan and Alan.

In (b) the coach and coachee are closer to one another, probably both psychologically and in the nature of the communication in the three-way relationship. It is easy in this situation for the sponsor, and the organisation more generally, to be positioned as the 'problem', and for the coach and coachee to collude in this and maybe defocus the coachee's contribution and responsibilities in the situation. Such a situation could have happened in the example above, perhaps if, after receiving a call inviting him to coach Alan, John met with Alan and agreed the agenda without properly engaging with Susan.

In (c) the coach and the sponsor are closer to one another, switching the dynamic of (b). Now it is the coachee who both coach and sponsor agree is the 'problem', and they are likewise likely to defocus the sponsor and organisational contribution to the situation. In our example, such a situation might develop if John takes away

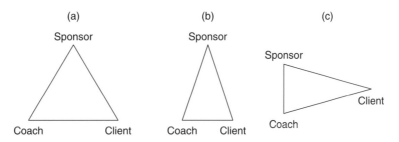

FIGURE 7.2   Aligning the coach–client–sponsor relationships

from his initial meeting with Susan that Alan is indeed the problem, a view that might be reinforced if John is keen to be regarded well by the organisation with an eye to future work.

It is easy to see that in (b) and (c) the relationships are skewed in ways that can fatally undermine the possibilities of a successful outcome to the coaching. The real issues will not be properly understood and addressed, and unhealthy dynamics of inclusion/exclusion, collusion, blame and so forth will almost certainly be present.

So what does this look like in practice? What happens after the three-way meeting? Let's pick up the story of John coaching Alan.

At the first coaching session they debrief the three-way meeting to confirm a shared understanding of the purpose and process of the coaching and then begin to explore, in line with our discussions in previous chapters, what is involved in how Alan relates to others, focusing particularly on his impact on other people. Though initially dismissive of the reaction of Susan and others, John does acknowledge that there is something familiar in what they are saying: family, friends and colleagues in previous organisations have said similar things. At the same time, his manner has been successful and appreciated by some, particularly people holding senior positions in organisations who see that he gets results, and they have promoted him on that basis. He feels quite ambivalent; he can see that the coaching is on to 'something' that's real, yet this 'something' has brought him success.

During this first session they agree on a number of key people that John can talk to to get informal 360-degree feedback, and also how Alan's coaching will be framed in those conversations (that he is having coaching to support him in his new role; he'd value feedback and suggestions to assist in this) and the kind of questions John will ask (for example: What's been most/least helpful in Alan's manner? What are the one or two things Alan could do that would most improve his involvement with you?). A consistent message comes back: yes, Alan gets results, but at a cost of alienating those around him, and the most important thing he can do is to find ways of influencing people that recognises what others are doing well: getting buy-in through appreciation and appropriate challenge rather than criticism.

John takes this feedback into the second session and underlines its significance for Alan and the coaching agenda. If Alan is to progress in the organisation it will be into more senior leadership positions, and a key attribute of such positions is the ability to influence others and build alliances, both those who report to him and also colleagues in the senior leadership team. His current manner is likely to undermine his chances of promotion or derail him if he gains promotion.

This is a challenging agenda for Alan as it goes to the heart of his ingrained behaviour patterns. It is also quite urgent, as it was agreed in the contracting that they will have a follow-up three-way meeting with Susan after four coaching sessions, to review progress. As a way forward Alan says he would like to focus on some current relationships that are particularly important, where he knows he has been critical, and work out ways of modifying his behaviour. John knows Alan likes reading, so suggests some books on 'emotional intelligence' and leadership to provide a rationale that John may find compelling, and which also concretely spell out some of the behaviours to aim for.

I hope you can see in the account so far that there are additional layers of complexity as the organisation becomes figural in the coaching. More people become involved, and care has to be taken in the contracting and subsequent processes to ensure that the interests of the various parties are given due weight. Acting in this way is vital for professional practice. It can also be vital if you are seeking to develop a business as a coach. Organisations that purchase coaching are increasingly aware of the importance of proper three-way contracting, as evidenced by the *Ridler Report* (Ridler & Co 2013). In the section entitled 'Indications and impressions which would persuade a coaching sponsor to include a coach on their preferred supplier list, when interviewing a coach', the statement 'Coach shows an interest in, and appreciation of, sponsor's organisation' was ranked the third most important factor (with an 88 per cent response), whilst the statement 'Coach gives sponsor confidence that they will balance organisation's goals and coachee's individual goals' was ranked fifth (with an 85 per cent response). It is clear, therefore, that a fundamental aspect of successful coaching in organisations is to ensure that the three-way contracting is properly in place and that there is an even-handed approach to the interests and agenda of both coach and sponsor.

2. OVERLAPPING RELATIONSHIPS

Coaching is often portrayed as a confidential relationship between two people in distinct roles (coach and coachee) who are not otherwise involved with each other, and it is this set-up which makes it safe for the coachee to work on very sensitive issues. Again this is reminiscent of the classic therapeutic relationship, where any involvements outside the relationship are usually viewed as detrimental to the therapy and likely to be unethical.

To get a sense of the importance of such a confidential set-up take a moment to imagine you are speaking to someone about something important to you, whilst knowing that:

- They have a vested interest in the outcome of the conversation.
- You may be involved with them again in a situation where what they know about you and their view of you will be important.
- They are involved with some of the important people you are talking about.

How would these circumstances influence the conversation?

I'm sure you can see that in this imagined scenario the conversation is likely to be very different to the kinds of confidential relationship we've discussed so far. Yet such shifts in the nature of the relationship are commonplace when coaching in organisations – so common that they become part of the 'ground', mostly taken for granted and not seen as particularly noteworthy. It is essential for us, however, given that our focus is the coaching relationship, to enquire a bit more deeply – make figural – who or what else may be present in that relationship and the impact the additional 'presences' may have.

Overlapping relationships mean being involved with a number of people who are also involved in some way with each other. For example, you may be an external coach coaching a number of people in the same leadership team, or perhaps you are an internal coach and your coachee is talking about other people you know and are involved with in the organisation. How does this involvement in multiple relationships change things?

Imagine you've been brought in to coach the CEO of an organisation, and also a number of people in the senior leadership team (a common enough situation in executive coaching). There is little doubt that they'll be talking about each other in the coaching, and you'll be hearing the many different views, concerns, alliances and plans of each. For example, David, the CEO, talks about his concerns with Joan the CFO. He's not sure if she is up to the job and whether he should replace her. You later meet Joan who is scathing about David, anxious about her future, and privately putting out feelers about posts outside the organisation. There are similar relational issues between other members of the team that you are coaching. Indeed, you are hearing about and involved with a network of people and their complex relationships with each other. How do you manage this? What if David tells you he has decided he is going to replace Joan but has not told her yet, and in your next session with Joan she says she's decided to make a go of her current role and wants to make this the focus of the coaching?

There is another dimension to this. The people in the senior team **know** that you are coaching the CEO and other members of the team. How do you think they regard you and your relationship with them and others? As a 'thought experiment', put yourself in the position of a member of that team. Imagine you are being coached by someone who is also coaching your colleagues and the CEO. What's that like for you? How might it impact upon the coaching relationship? Of course, each person will have their own reaction, founded in part on the culture of the team (e.g. a high level of trust versus a divided, hostile grouping), on their personal and professional history (perhaps growing up in a large family with lots of rivalry between siblings) and their own ambitions, but I'd predict the likelihood of certain kinds of concerns. What are others saying about me? Who does the coach believe: me or others? Who is the 'favourite' coachee? What does the coach know that she's holding back on? The situation is a playground for anxiety, fantasy, speculation and imagination.

The complexity of this situation is illustrated in Figure 7.3, where the coach is working with a number of people in the same team, though in reality it is not possible to illustrate the extent of this complexity.

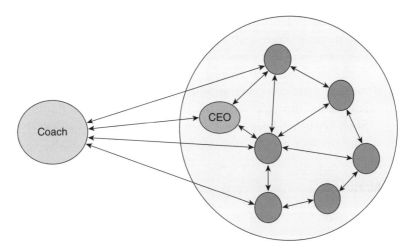

FIGURE 7.3   The web of overlapping relationships

Given that your coachees know you are coaching others in the team, what else might happen? It's likely you'll find yourself playing a part in the politics of the team. Knowing that others will be putting their own point of view across, your coachees may want to convince you of their side of the story. You might also be 'used' to pass messages within the team. Some of this, of course, happens out of awareness, the kind of unconscious process that is naturally evoked in group settings. In effect, you've become part of the system whether you are aware of it or not, and it's not possible to be unaffected by it. In a way, Figure 7.3 should perhaps be redrawn with the coach situated within the team, rather than positioned externally. Here is one small example of this process.

In the morning I am coaching Jason, who is struggling with his job, knowing that his performance has dropped off, partly, he says (though not solely), because of the style of management of his new manager Alison, who is in his view very 'hands on', micromanaging and not respecting that he's been doing the job well for a number of years. He is seeking some recognition from Alison of what he's achieved and his current expertise, and wanting more help from her with strategic thinking. Feeling criticised and unappreciated he is, to some extent, 'taking his bat and ball home', even though he recognised this could damage him.

I know that he knows I am coaching Alison in the afternoon, and sure enough her agenda is about Jason's performance. She is becoming increasingly frustrated with him. She sees him as arrogant and lazy and intends to performance-manage him in a very close way. Being a 'participant observer' of this *folie à deux* is extremely difficult, and reflecting upon it later I come to the view that, in a sense, Jason was setting me up or inviting me to carry a message to his manager about what he needed and what she could do to get the best out of him.

I don't think Jason was consciously seeking to influence me, and I believe there was positive intention behind what he was saying. Nevertheless, on reflection I'm pretty sure that I was caught up in their relational issues and that my coaching in the afternoon was shaped, in some measure and out of my awareness, by the message I was carrying, maybe helping Alison to view the situation differently and think through some alternative strategies to performance management. Such dynamics, I suggest, are the norm rather than an exception when coaching a network of people who are involved with each other.

3. DUAL ROLES

By dual roles I mean the situation where you are occupying more than one role in the relationship, though that additional role may be in the background. Some examples might be:

- A coach with a business development role, i.e. coaching with a mindset of developing further commercial opportunities.
- One-to-one and team coaching the same group of people.
- Managing and coaching direct reports.
- An internal coach whose 'day job' is in HR or OD (organisational development).
- Providing coach training and one-to-one coaching.

> Take a moment to consider for yourself the likely significance of dual roles:
>
> - You are about to begin a new coaching relationship with a senior person in a large organisation.
> - You believe that if the coaching goes well it will lead to more work.
> - How do you think this commercial consideration will impact upon the coaching relationship?

Let's explore a couple of these situations to see what influence dual roles may have on the coaching relationship.

COACHING AND BUSINESS DEVELOPMENT

Such dual purpose is common for the external coach, so much a normal part of the 'ground' in coaching that its significance may be overlooked and hard to grasp. The difference is likely to be most figural when you first make the shift from pro bono to paid coaching, before it becomes the norm; indeed, the whole territory can seem to be refashioned once money enters the scene. As a coach you're likely to feel the need to 'sell yourself' on the coaching market, putting together an impressive CV and perhaps participating in the 'beauty parade' matching coaches to coachees. You'll have much more of a stake in the outcome of the work – in it being 'successful':

- Are you listening out for the tantalising prospect of more work, particularly if you're just starting up, or if you're working for an organisation where business development is expected as part of your role?
- Do you feel under pressure to come up with 'a result' when you're being paid for the work? And does how much you charge become an issue in itself – a reflection, perhaps, of your sense of personal and professional worth?
- Will your practice change in other ways? For example, how prepared are you to challenge the coachee if it is likely to displease them, particularly if they are a person in a position of seniority and influence?

There was that evocative and challenging question 'Where were all the coaches when the banks went down?' (Whitmore et al. 2009), alerting us to the possibilities of colluding with practices we may feel uncomfortable about if the challenge involves commercial risk.

Of course, some of the things I'm writing about here may be present in pro bono work as well, but there is no doubt that something new and powerful enters the relationship when there is a commercial element to the work. In the Introduction I quoted O'Connor and Lages: 'In many ways business coaching is the human potential movement gone corporate' (2007). The questions being raised here are about the influence of the 'corporate' in the coaching relationship. I'd invite you to think for yourself about that influence, particularly if you are now setting up, or have set up, as an external coach.

INTERNAL COACH WITH OTHER ROLES IN THE ORGANISATION

The role of internal coach brings with it some of the greatest challenges around overlapping and dual roles (St John-Brooks 2013). The most frequent set-up is that someone who has their own 'day job' in the organisation gains additional training as a coach and joins the coaching resource offering coaching to other people in the organisation.

As an internal coach it will be quite common for you to hear from coachees about people that are of interest, because you know them or because of their role in the organisation. Indeed, you may hear about people and situations that directly impact upon your role. It may be that you are in HR and you discover that a complaint has been made against your coachee and it's hard for you not to be involved. Or you are in OD and an organisational change is in the offing which has not yet been announced but will significantly affect your coachee, who, for example, may be working on an agenda that will soon become irrelevant. It is also likely that you will already have your own opinions, feelings, beliefs and involvements with people and situations your coachee is talking about, and find yourself comparing what you are hearing to your own experience.

MANAGING OVERLAPPING RELATIONSHIPS AND DUAL ROLES

Overlapping relationships and dual roles have been discussed separately, but often, of course, both situations are in play at the same time, particularly for the internal coach, where you may be hearing about many other people you are involved with, and what you are hearing about has implications for your other role(s). These difficulties and dilemmas pose some of the most challenging situations that you'll encounter, situations that, paradoxically, most coaches regard as 'normal' because in a sense they are the 'ground', part of the everyday experience of coaching in organisations. Such normality can still make its presence felt, however, perhaps as background anxiety and confusion – a sense of unease that things aren't 'right'; maybe feeling somehow compromised in relations with others; or a realisation that things have got out of shape and are in danger of derailing.

What is your experience here? Bring to mind situations where you are involved in overlapping relationships and dual roles:

- What challenges did they pose?
- How did you manage the situations?
- What are your thoughts on how you will go about managing overlapping and dual roles in coaching?

How can we proceed in such situations? Are there any frameworks and guidelines to provide direction? The first thing to acknowledge is that, in the main, coaching has not yet developed (and may never develop) the theoretical and professional resources to give clear guidance in such situations because they are just so complex. The codes of ethics are helpful; for example the European Mentoring and Coaching Council (2008) *Code of Ethics* says about boundary management that the coach will:

> be aware of the potential for conflicts of interest of either a commercial or emotional nature to arise through the coach/mentoring relationship and deal with them quickly and effectively to ensure there is no detriment to the coachee or sponsor.

And in relation to professionalism, that he or she will:

> not exploit the coachee in any manner, including, but not limited to, financial, sexual or those matters within the professional relationship. The coach/mentor will ensure that the duration of the coach/mentoring contract is only as long as is necessary for the coachee/sponsor.

Similar statements are made in the codes of other professional bodies, and they provide a useful framework to address gross misconduct, but are harder to apply in the kind of situations we've been addressing. Where, for example, is the line between legitimate business development and financial exploitation? How do you manage the information you're getting from other coachees or other contacts?

The golden rule in the earlier section on 'Who is the client' is contracting, and this is always the foundation for establishing good practice; but the kinds of situations we've been discussing tend to 'go under the radar' of contracting, perhaps because they are so much part of the 'ground' and thus inextricably interwoven with taken-for-granted everyday coaching practice. What then is the basis for good practice?

The fundamental and mostly unrecognised source of good practice, which comes from outside the profession of coaching per se, is the awareness and skills we've developed in everyday life, from the day we are born, to operate effectively in social situations, including managing overlapping relationships and dual roles – with families, friends and colleagues. We develop the capacity to hold confidences, to manage the awkwardness of the unspoken even when it is relevant to the current conversation. This tacit knowledge, which we are mostly unaware of and apply with hardly a thought, forms the foundation, I believe, of our professional practice in this area. It is what enables us to 'find our way around', and is the basis upon which we build as we gain experience in coaching and refine this tacit knowledge. The other professional resources we bring, such as the codes of ethics, works on the basis of this tacit knowledge, enabling us for instance to make sense of and make judgements about 'exploitation'.

The second source of good practice is your growing sense of what constitutes the proper coaching frame and process – the overall integrity of the coaching relationship which now includes not only the coachee but also the organisation, in the person of sponsor and others who are involved. When supervising coaches this is a fundamental thing I'm always listening out for: the integrity of the process.

Many of the issues coaches bring to supervision involve difficulties in this area, with unclear boundaries, conflict in roles, and so forth. It is worth noting that many (probably most) people you are involved with in organisations don't understand coaching and you'll have to manage and to some extent educate them in the ways of coaching. For example, the manager of a coachee may want you to tell them how it's going, without a clear understanding of confidentiality, and get quite cross and frustrated at your refusal to share details of the work.

There will be judgements to be made as to whether current or anticipated coaching is actually viable, or whether the circumstances undermine the integrity of the process and thus the possibilities of proper and ethical coaching. For example, is it OK to coach the CEO and members of her senior leadership team? You need to consider the relational complexity of such an arrangement. If you answer yes to that question, you may then need to consider how many of the senior leadership team you can properly coach — just some, or all of them? Where is the balance between commercial interest and the integrity of the coaching process? An area that has received particular attention is whether it is possible as a manager to coach direct reports (where coaching is a formal set-up rather than using coaching skills as a style of management), as the issues of power, authority and dual role become particularly intense. A CIPD report concludes:

> There appeared to be a consensus within the HR teams setting up development opportunities for line managers that the psychological boundary issues for line managers formally 'coaching' their own staff are very difficult to manage. Even if organisations begin with the intention of having 'coaching' as a separate activity for line managers with their teams, we haven't yet found any organisations that have done it successfully. This supports the conventional wisdom and professional standards which say that the roles and responsibilities of line management make formally 'coaching' your own staff very difficult. (Knights 2008, p. 7)

This example shows that there are constraints and limitations on the viability of coaching, though the line between what is and is not feasible is not always self-evident; there are some people who would argue that it is possible for a line manager to formally coach their direct reports, and do so themselves.

The third source of good practice is supervision. The situations we are dealing with here are so complex and difficult to think and feel through that supervision is a necessary and vital space in order to reach the kind of clarity needed to work effectively. The supervisor can help you:

- Pay attention to the messiness that is almost certainly going to be present.
- Do what is required to get the proper coaching frame and process in place.
- Explore the kind of relationships that are developing between you, the coachee, the sponsor and the wider organisation.
- Address the complexity of the overlapping relationships and duality of roles, and explore the impact these are having on the coaching relationships.
- Address the likely ethical issues that will arise through your involvement with such a complex web of roles and relationships.

Overall then, we can see that the step from pro bono coaching to paid coaching within organisations is a big step that significantly increases the relational complexity of the work. In a similar way to when you first started coaching, you can expect to be less than sure-footed at the beginning and be uncertain at times. Be aware that the process is likely to be, by its very nature, messy at times, and that the inevitable confusion and uncertainty is not all down to you. At the same time, being clear about the principles of good practice can act as a compass in the work. These include:

- Contracting properly with both the coachee and sponsor and with others involved in the coaching.
- Being even-handed with all concerned.
- Being proactive where necessary in educating people about coaching and setting up appropriate relationships.
- Attending to the various elements that are likely to be required in the process, such as 360-degree feedback, reviewing progress and evaluating the coaching.
- Being aware of the impact of overlapping relationships and dual roles.
- Using supervision to get clear about what is happening and the way forward.

From the very first engagement with organisations you'll learn fast, building upon the tacit knowledge you already have, supplementing it with your professional understanding and developing a practice where you have a sense of knowing your way around. Having said this, you'll *always* encounter messiness, and be challenged by complex situations that can feel awkward and raise anxiety, and which require supervision to enable you to get clarity and an understanding of the next step.

Getting the next step right can be vital. A colleague of mine, who coaches primarily in national and multinational corporations, put it this way: his reputation as a coach, and therefore his future business, depend fundamentally on trust – a trust built on properly managing relations with coachees and sponsors – and doing the right thing, even when this may displease someone who, for instance, asks him to break a confidence or take a course of action outside the proper frame of the coaching process. Going along with such requests can bring short-term gain and relief, but others take notice of what happens, and once lost, trust is hard to regain.

IMPLICATIONS FOR PRACTICE

We have covered a lot of ground in this chapter and have the opportunity here to gather up some of the strands. Take some time to consider for yourself:

- Your understanding of three-way contracting, being even-handed with all parties, and the other elements you'll need to contract for when coaching in organisations.
- How you have managed with overlapping and dual relationships in aspects of your life other than coaching (e.g. as a manager and colleague to people at work, or in the middle of disputes between family/friends)?
- Based upon your experience of overlapping relationships and dual roles, are there any guidelines and resources for helping you manage such situations?

RECOMMENDED READING

St John-Brooks (2013) *Internal Coaching: The Inside Story* is a good book for getting a feel for the kind of situations and challenges thrown up by overlapping and dual relationships.

Bluckert (2006) *Psychological Dimension of Executive Coaching*. 'Part 1: A framework for effective coaching' goes into some detail about good coaching processes when coaching in organisations, and what he calls the 'critical success factors in executive coaching'.

8

Supervision and Personal Development

Take a moment to think about what the word **supervision** means to you. What feelings or thoughts does it evoke?

For many people, based upon their experience in other places, supervision has the connotation of authority, of command and control: being monitored, checked up on, maybe being observed to make sure you're doing things correctly. There is an element of authority and 'quality control' in coaching supervision but, as we shall see, this is set within a context that frames the practice very differently.

Coaching supervision is primarily about providing a safe reflective space where you can share your practice with someone who knows about coaching and is often more experienced in the field, with the intention of deepening your understanding of coaching and developing your capability to work more effectively. It is also a place to contain and work through the anxieties, uncertainties and confusions that arise in coaching, something I'm guessing you're already familiar with.

You might ask: if supervision is a loaded word that may set up a misleading view of the practice, why use it? Why not find a better word? I've been in various forums and discussion groups where this has been tried, coming up with formulations such as 'coaching the coach', or 'mentoring the coach', or 'coach consultation', but we discover that every alternative word carries its own 'baggage', its own connotations, and to date every such discussion has gone full circle and settled on 'supervision' as the word to use.

In the early days of coaching (which, remember, was not so long ago – around the mid-1990s) there was considerable disagreement about the place and purpose of supervision. You'll be aware that there are many roots to coaching: for example, sport, organisational development, HR, adult learning, organisational and clinical psychology, counselling and psychotherapy. For people from most of these professions there was no tradition and obvious place for supervision in their practice, so why have it in coaching? The primary impetus for supervision came from those with a counselling and psychotherapy background, in which supervision is integral to professional practice. For a number of years the message was that supervision is 'nice to have' but not a requirement. Recently, however, the professional bodies (ICF, EMCC, AC) have made regular supervision a requirement for ethical practice and necessary for accreditation, and this is transforming the place of supervision in coaching, from being peripheral to central to practice. This shift is particularly challenging for organisations, many of whom have trained large numbers of coaches and now find that the additional provision of supervision is required; how to do this in a professional and cost-effective way is the question.

The fundamental case for supervision (which you can test out for yourself) is that the work we do is so complex – involving individual, interpersonal and organisational relationships, all of which may involve strong emotion – that a place is needed to think and feel through all that is involved. Supervision is, first and foremost, for the benefit and protection of the coachee because coaching is a professional service, and the well-being and development of the coachee its primary purpose. However, supervision is also about the well-being and development of the coach, and it's my view that 'resourcing' and supporting the coach also benefits and safeguards the coachee.

To set the scene let's have a look at some frameworks and approaches to supervision, and how supervision may enter into and impact upon your relationships with coachees. We'll then look at how you can prepare for and make the best use of supervision sessions.

THE FUNCTIONS OF SUPERVISION

One useful way to approach supervision is to consider its functions. A number of people (Kadushin 1976; Proctor 1988; Hawkins and Smith 2013; de Haan 2012) have identified three primary functions, which they have described using different terms, but which cover much the same ground (see Figure 8.1).

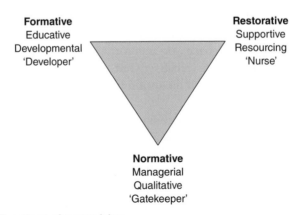

Formative
Educative
Developmental
'Developer'

Restorative
Supportive
Resourcing
'Nurse'

Normative
Managerial
Qualitative
'Gatekeeper'

FIGURE 8.1 Functions of supervision

Formative. Paying attention to the formative function, the supervisor will focus on developing your professional capabilities as a coach, in terms, for example, of your theoretical understanding, your skills, the significance of what you are bringing into the coaching relationship, dealing with ethical issues and so forth. Your supervisor will very much be building on the learning from your programme, and it is important that they have an understanding of what you are covering in the workshops. It is also a place to consider your own future as a coach: for example, professional accreditation and the development of your career as a coach.

Restorative. Coaching is demanding work, and effective practice requires that you be open to and emotionally available to the coachee and their situation. By its very nature coaching invites you into a field of strong emotion – it is often uplifting and exciting, sometimes anxiety-provoking, confusing and frustrating. Such work can be quite 'depleting' and quite wearing, and supervision is a place to rebuild resilience and a relationship in which you can regain a sense of well-being. The opportunity to share your experience of the coaching relationship and how you are feeling, with someone who 'knows the territory' and can help you work through and make sense of what is going on, can be enormously helpful in building confidence. The supervisor can be thought of as a 'secure base' (Bowlby 2005), someone who is 'there' if and when things get difficult: someone who is on your side and has your welfare at heart.

Normative. One way that supervision differs from coaching is that the role of supervisor carries with it professional authority. The supervisor is the 'guardian of the integrity of the coaching process' – integrity in terms of what is ethical and also in terms of keeping the proper boundaries/frame to the work. The concept of 'good authority' (Pitt-Aikens and Thomas Ellis 1990) was mentioned in Chapter 2 as a notion that is particularly important in supervision. It can be very empowering and reassuring to be in the presence of someone who comfortably embodies good authority, particularly when that person is a supervisor. She may draw attention to/challenge you around ethical issues, diversity, proper boundaries or contracting, such that you leave a supervision session feeling your practice is in good shape or you know what to do to improve it.

FORMS OF SUPERVISION

It is likely that you'll participate in differing forms of supervision, so it will be useful to outline them briefly.

One-to-one supervision

Here you meet with a supervisor who most likely has qualifications in both coaching and supervision – a practitioner with more experience than you, whom you meet on an agreed regular basis. I say most likely, because supervision is still quite new in coaching, and finding a supervisor who is also a coach is often not easy. For a transition period, until there are more coaches with supervision training, it may be that you find someone who has training in supervision but not coaching (for example, someone with a therapeutic background). It is likely that your coaching programme has a network of supervisors that you can draw from. However the connection is made, it's good to spend some time finding out about the supervisor's background so see how this meets your needs.

Group supervision

Here, as the name suggests, you meet as a member of a group, again led ideally by a supervisor with experience as a coach and supervisor. Such groups can be run in different ways, depending upon the approach of the supervisor. Some, in effect, do one-to-one supervision in a group setting, with participants taking turns to talk through the material with the supervisor, with other group members in the background. Other supervisors like to include group members more in the process, inviting them to ask questions, share observations and so forth.

Group supervision brings additional complexity which needs to be addressed, particularly at the contracting phase. How is the group to be run and what is the role of the supervisor and group members in the process? There are likely to be additional issues of confidentiality, particularly when you know group members from other settings, and it is particularly challenging if (as often happens) you work in the same or related organisations. Logistically, how is time going to be managed if there are more participants wanting to bring material than the time available? (As a rule of thumb I reckon at least 30–40 minutes is required for each presentation.) What are the 'rules of engagement' if there is whole-group participation in the supervision? It can happen that everyone gets so interested that the person presenting gets bombarded by others' interventions, and this has to be properly managed through agreeing at the contracting phase on how members of the group will behave towards each other in the sessions.

Peer supervision

With peer supervision you contract with another coach to supervise each other, taking turns in each role. This can be a very cost- and time-efficient way of working, and can have a strong developmental edge, as you take on the role of supervisor. It also addresses one of the key features of the usual one-to-one and group supervision set-up – the power differential between supervisor and coach, which almost inevitably has an impact on the dynamics of the relationship (perhaps evoking transference feelings around authority and expertise). The downside to peer supervision, particularly when you are in the early stages of development as a coach, is precisely the lack of experience in the supervision–coach 'system', as you will both be working on the basis of your current understanding of coaching. Alongside this, perhaps because the set-up may seem more informal with a sense that 'we are both in this together' and perhaps co-participants on a programme, an element of collusiveness may be present which limits the scope for challenge. During the early stages of learning your 'craft' as a coach, peer supervision is very much to be encouraged, but as an addition to and not an alternative to one-on-one or group supervision with an experienced supervisor.

'Virtual' supervision

Virtual supervision involves using the phone or online video such as Skype. People have differing views as to the impact of using virtual forms, some much preferring face-to-face, others arguing that phone or video has much to offer. Whatever one's position on this, there is no doubt that virtual communication has become part of everyday practice whether we are engaged in coaching or supervision, and it is important to get experience of both in developing your capability as a coach. I do believe that during your initial training it is important to have predominantly face-to-face supervision. This will enable you to build a better relationship with your supervisor, and a great deal of the tacit relational knowing that is at the heart of coaching and supervision will be more fully present face-to-face, though some argue that you become more sensitised to specific channels of communication in virtual supervision, for example attuning more closely to the dimensions of voice on the phone (Murdoch 2008). It may be that you choose to experiment, for example with peer supervision, some of which is face to face and some by phone or video conferencing.

A MODEL OF SUPERVISION

As with coaching, there are various models of supervision. There is one model that is very popular, and it is likely that if your supervisor has been trained in supervision they will know and probably use it: Hawkins and Smith's (2013) seven-eyed process model of supervision (Figure 8.2), a model first developed for therapy (Hawkins and Shohet 2012). It will be good for you to be familiar with the model, as it may enable you to have a common framework within which you and your supervisor can work. Also, it is a model that fits with the purpose of this book: the seven eyes are various lenses to systematically review the relational dynamics in coaching and supervision. In working through the model we'll gather up many of the threads of the previous chapters, offering the opportunity to integrate the various perspectives and systematically pay attention to some of the relational dynamics you'll encounter.

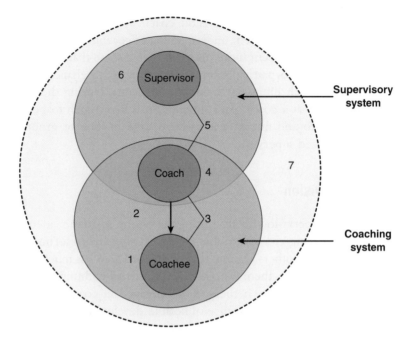

FIGURE 8.2 The seven-eyed process model of supervision

A fundamental feature of the model is that it maps out and explores the dynamics of overlapping systems. In the model there is the 'coaching system' and the 'supervision system', both of them separate systems with the coach as a bridge between them. The coach is a participant in both systems and in a very real sense carries the dynamics of each system back and forth: from the coaching system into the supervision system and (very importantly) from the supervision system back into the coaching system. Both systems in turn are set within the 'system' of the wider world, indicated by the outer dotted circle.

In what follows we will go through the seven eyes and see how they connect with what we have been exploring in previous chapters. But before we do that one important caveat is required: each 'eye' can be spoken about as if it is distinct, but in reality they are abstractions from the various systems/relationships, which are, in fact, constitutive of each 'eye'. For example, I cannot describe the coachee as a separate distinct entity separate from my own upbringing, training, intention and so forth. Each such 'eye' is relational through and through. Nevertheless, and with that caveat in mind, there is value in attending to each 'eye'.

Eye 1: the coachee

Here we attend to the coachee, and you'll be telling your supervisor the story of what brings the coachee to coaching: what you know about them, their work and non-work situation, what they want from coaching, how they present in the session (eager, reticent), and maybe what they look and sound like. You are, in a sense, bringing the coachee into the room and very concretely describing what you see.

This may sound like a straightforward thing to do but it's not. I strongly recommend that you read Shainberg's (1983) paper, describing how a supervisor helps a practitioner get past their preconceptions, interpretations, self-doubts and unstated demands on a coachee, which is preventing him seeing the coachee, and the very moving moment when he truly recognises the client as a person, and not just as a 'client' who is a threat to professional capability. It would be nice to say that the anxieties and tactics of the practitioner in Shainberg's paper are aspects of something that happens whilst people are in training, a phase which we get past. However, this is definitely not the case. We are all, always, susceptible to the anxieties that evoke such tactics. In fact, as we become more experienced the temptation can grow to 'cut corners', thinking we understand because what we are hearing seems so familiar.

Alongside the dynamics Shainberg describes, some interesting and important things can come from this focus on the coachee: it may be that you struggle to describe the coachee's appearance or haven't got a real sense of their 'presence' in the room; maybe certain things stand out whilst other things, which should be obvious, aren't clear ('Do you know, though we seemed to talk about it, I realise I have no real idea of why they've come to coaching'). As well as your own filters there may be something about *how* the coachees brings themselves into the room which is important and emerges through paying close attention to the session. You'll quickly see that relational issues are present from the first moment of contact with the coachee, and it is in the supervision space that awareness can be raised of what you've noticed but have not yet clearly articulated.

It is with this 'eye' that you can also reflect upon the coachee's 'self-management' strategies, as discussed in Chapter 2. What are they anxious about? What are the underlying conflicts? What are the 'creative adjustments' that have become 'fixed gestalts' – ways of behaving that can be both strengths and limitations (what got them to 'here' but won't get them to 'there')? How can you work with them to enable the optimal anxiety for productive work?

Eye 2: the coaching interventions

Here we are exploring our interventions with the coachee, such as the use of open questions, paraphrasing and so on, with the intention of reviewing their appropriateness and exploring different options.

This can be an anxiety-raising 'eye' particularly if you're on a programme, where the question 'Am I doing it right?' can be figural, and the supervisor, with more experience and in a position of power, has the capability (and may feel drawn) to pass judgement on the merits of your work. Notice how you are around your supervisor. Are you anticipating judgement? Are you looking to them to tell you what to do? Or are you able to hold your own sense of being 'good enough' and engage in an open conversation about your coaching?

This 'eye' is fertile ground for 'parallel process', where the dynamics of one system are carried into and played out in another system. For example, we've said throughout that the heart of coaching is the belief that the coachee has the capability to find their own way forward: 'ask not tell'. This belief can be severely tested when the coaching feels stuck, or you're lacking confidence as a coach and the coachee is looking for answers. In such circumstances there is a strong temptation as the coach to revert to 'tell', to give you a sense of offering something worthwhile to the coachee. If such a dynamic is at play then there is the likelihood that you'll approach supervision in the same spirit and seek to get your supervisor to tell you what to do. After all, they are the expert with answers: so (without deliberately setting out to do so) you may play the same 'game' with your supervisor as was played in the coaching. Hopefully the supervisor will not get drawn into responding by tell, but rather invite curiosity, exploration and self-evaluation; in other words, take a coaching approach in supervision. If this happens, then again by parallel process, it's likely you'll hold more firmly to a coaching approach to your coachee.

You can see that there is a lot at stake with this second 'eye', and there is a lot to learn if you can hold an awareness of how you are entering supervision. It's also worth noting that, for whatever reason, your supervisor may be in tell mode, which can be enticing and you may be hearing lots of interesting, valuable insights. Just be cautious about how you take this back into the coaching relationship; parallel process is subtle and works both ways, often affecting our manner with coachees in ways we are hardly aware of. Having been 'told', there is a distinct possibility you'll re-enter coaching in a tell mode.

Eye 3: the coaching relationship

Here we are exploring the coaching relationship, primarily from the perspective of what the coachee is bringing into the relationship (the coach's contribution is explored in Eye 4).

This focus lines up with the notions of 'relationship management' and transference, explored in Chapter 4, of how the coachee incorporates the coaching relationship into their familiar style of relating. The supervisor will help you take a step back from the specific details of the session and reflect on how you and the coachee are as a 'couple', perhaps inviting you to come up with an image or metaphor to catch how you are together ('Well it seems like a wrestling match'; 'I'm kind of waiting to be told off'; 'I feel like the saviour – the best person the coachee's ever met'). In addition to the coachee's familiar style of relating, it's likely that parallel process will also be present: in this instance some aspect of systems the coachee is part of, for example the culture of their workplace, which they are carrying into and replaying in the relationship with you.

We've seen in our discussion of relationship management that getting a grasp of these relational dynamics can be vital to the success of the coaching and possibly transformational for the coachee. In supervision you can catch hold of these dynamics, seek to understand their significance in terms of the coach's agenda, consider how to raise the coachee's awareness of the dynamics, and explore ways of working to enable the coachee to change their behaviour so as to attain their stated goals more effectively.

Eye 4: the coach

This 'eye' is perhaps the most complex of all as it focuses on you in two roles at the same time – as coach in the coaching system and as supervisee in the supervision system. The additional complexity is that you are also the 'bridge' between the two systems, by means of which the dynamics of each system travel in a process of reciprocal influence.

The coach system
As the coach in the coach–coachee relationship, there are a number of facets to attend to:

- Your countertransference to the coachee, which we explored in Chapter 4. What reaction is being evoked in you in response to the coachee's relationship management strategies? How can this reaction be used to understand the coachee and the impact they have on others, particularly in relation to the coachee's agenda?
- Your own relationship management strategies. What are these, how do they help shape the coaching relationship, and how do they sync with the countertransference response? It's vital that you develop self-awareness as to our own contribution to the coaching relationship – you are 50 per cent of all that happens. Without this understanding it is easy to attribute all which happens in the coaching relationship to the personality and behaviour of the coachee (who can then become the source of both the transference and countertransference behaviour). The objectivity you gain through concretely describing the coachee in Eye 1 can be an important reference point for gauging your own contribution to the relationship.

- Your response to the parallel process carried into the session by the coachee, as discussed earlier.
- The cultural identities of you and the coachee, and issues of culture, difference and diversity which will be present in the coaching relationship.

The supervision system

As the supervisee in the supervisee–supervisor relationship, there are a number of facets that mirror the coach system dynamics:

- Your transference to the supervisor who, being in a position of power and authority, is likely to evoke considerable transference in supervisees. Check in with yourself around this. What is your response to your supervisor? Are there any familiar patterns, in terms of relating to authority figures or in how you are relating to her (e.g. anxiety about making mistakes; desire to please)?
- Your usual self-management strategies, of which transference is an aspect. Again, check in with yourself. How are you bringing yourself into the supervision relationship and how does that shape what then happens?
- Is there a parallel process in the supervision relationship? Are you carrying something from the coaching system into the supervision system?
- Your cultural identity and your reaction to the cultural identity of the supervisor. What is the place of difference and diversity in your relationship?

Eyes 5 and 6: supervisor focus on supervision relationship

Eyes 5 and 6 are less available for us to work with as a coach. The seven-eyed model was developed for supervisors, and these 'eyes' are concerned with the supervisor focusing (Eye 5) on the supervision relationship and (Eye 6) on their own experience in the supervision relationship. Eyes 5 and 6 mirror the coach attending to Eyes 3 and 4 in the coaching system.

Though they are less available to work with as a coach, these 'eyes', particularly Eye 5, are still useful for raising awareness, particularly awareness of the supervision relationship. We've already covered some of this ground, as it is through this lens that we attend to parallel process and to other aspects such as difference and diversity. More generally Eye 5 invites reflection on 'how we are doing in the supervision relationship', and you can take an active role in this. For example, is the contract between you clear? Are you getting what you want from supervision? What are you noticing in the 'here and now' of the supervision relationship? Active use of the model helps us pay attention to the supervision relationship, not just go along with it, which can greatly enhance its value. Furthermore, in terms of parallel process, you being active in the supervision relationship in the way described is likely to free up the coachee to take a similar stance in relation to you in the coaching relationship – that is the nature of parallel process.

Eye 7: the wider context

This is an important 'eye', bringing into focus that which can so easily be overlooked when absorbed in attending to the coaching relationship. All our work, for coachee, coach and supervisor, is shaped and structured by the context – the 'field' – in which it is embedded, as we explored in Chapter 5.

Hawkins and Smith (2013) identify and discuss seven foci for Eye 7, moving systematically out from the workplace to key stakeholders and to global issues. Rather than review these seven foci here I'd encourage you to read Hawkins and Smith's account. To give a flavour, though, of the importance of the context consider the impact of government policies with regard to the NHS, education, social services in the public sector, and new regimes of regulation in the financial sector and other utilities such as power and transport. The effects of these policies often saturate the coaching agenda, though their impact can so easily be overlooked if the focus is primarily on the coachee and their way of engaging with issues.

It's also worth considering the wider context for us as coaches and how this impacts on the coaching relationship. Coaching is a profession, a way of making a living: perhaps self-employed, perhaps part of an organisation offering coaching, or perhaps as part of a role within an organisation. In each of these positions it will be important to be 'successful', in whatever way this is defined. For example, if I am self-employed I'll be concerned that the coaching goes well for my reputation and probably hoping for some repeat business. With this as the background maybe I know I should challenge a senior leader about their behaviour around racism or sexuality, but be anxious that I'll jeopardise our relationship and future work together. Or again, maybe someone who commissions coaching for an important coachee organisation wants a conversation 'offline' about the coaching I'm doing with one of their employees. Whatever you do, this wider context is crucially part of the field; you have to include your own setting, your practice, when considering Eye 7.

MAKING THE MOST OF SUPERVISION

Working through the seven-eyed model reveals the complexity of the work we do, and the importance of supervision becomes self-evident. Once you've had supervision you'll probably wonder how you could practice without it, as it is such an invaluable space for reflection. Given its importance, the question arises regarding how to make the most out of supervision. The parallel (and the parallel process) with the coaching relationship is easy to see: how you bring yourself into the supervision relationship and what happens in that relationship will resonate with how you are with coachees in the coaching relationship.

Consider the kind of relationship you'd like to establish with your supervisor:

- How would you like to be in that relationship?
- What are the qualities you are looking for in the supervisor?
- How safe do you feel to honestly share your doubts, concerns and uncertainties?
- If you are already in supervision, what image or metaphor captures the nature of the relationship between you and your supervisor?

I'll give you some of my thinking around this. My ideal picture is of two (or more in group supervision) practitioners, in different roles, who have a sense of shared ownership of and responsibility for the relationship. Again we have something that seems simple but is not necessarily easy to achieve, primarily because of the dynamics of power and authority in the relationship – dynamics that are most prevalent if you are in training or relatively new to coaching. In this situation the supervisor can seem like the embodiment of professional expertise and standards, which, along with the authority of their position, is a virtual playground for transference.

It's inevitable that the power and authority of the supervisor will have an impact, and it's worth taking a moment to reflect on how you respond in such situations: perhaps deferential, anxious to please, somewhat rebellious or ready to challenge. The language of transactional analysis that we discussed previously can help here. The stance to aspire to is 'I'm OK – you're OK' – we are both resourceful, capable people engaged in a shared task to which we both contribute. The contrast is 'I'm not OK – you're OK', in other words (from the supervisee position), the supervisor is someone better than me, superior to me (the more deferential position); or perhaps 'I'm OK – you're not OK', the more combative position where the underlying strategy is to dismiss the supervisor and what they have to offer. In reality there is the likelihood of switching from one position to another.

The language of TA (transactional analysis) is good here because you can simply and directly check out what state you're in, and if you're not in the preferred state reflect on what is happening and how to get back to the 'I'm OK – you're OK' position. It might be, for example, that there is something about the supervisor's tone of voice that leaves you feeling criticised, feeling not OK, and you need to check this out to get back to being OK. The mantra of 'I'm OK – you're OK' constantly draws you towards being a resourceful, capable 'adult' in the relationship.

It's important, then, to be aware of your state of mind vis-à-vis the supervisor. Here are some thoughts on practical things to do to make the most of supervision.

Finding a supervisor

It is important, when choosing a supervisor, to:

- Be choice-full. Identify a number of possible supervisors and check out their backgrounds – their career, their coaching and supervision experience and approach, perhaps their cultural profile. It might be you'd like a supervisor with a background in something you feel is 'missing' from your own experience. Perhaps you have always worked in fast-paced, performance-focused businesses and would like a supervisor who can help you with the psychological dimension, or you may have a psychological background and would value a supervisor with a strong organisational understanding.
- Have an initial 'chemistry' meeting with a number of people before you settle on someone who feels right for you. Take some time to get to know each other – share about yourself and maybe invite the supervisor to do the same.
- Spend time on agreeing the contract: confidentiality, fee, time, place, frequency, missed sessions and so on. The way you go about this, and then what happens subsequently involving the contract (e.g. whether you hold to the agreement if you miss sessions), will play powerfully into how you contract with your coachees.

Having begun supervision

Once supervision has begun, make sure that you:

- Prepare for a supervision session. Identify the coachees you'd like to discuss, have the coachees fresh in your mind and be clear about why you are bringing each coachee. This preparation is likely to give you a sense of being ready for the session and confident in yourself.
- Check in as to whether there is something particular you'd like to get from a session. Maybe there are aspects of your practice you'd like to focus on and develop – e.g. use of self, getting a better grasp on organisational dynamics or the psychological dimension of coaching.
- Review the sessions with your supervisor. How are you getting on with each other? What's going well, not so well? What would enhance your work together?
- Are courageous in being honest about things that have happened that you are embarrassed about because you seem to have done badly in the session. Maybe you've found that with one coachee you keep giving advice, and cannot stop doing it; maybe with another coachee you've not been able to hold proper

boundaries, allowing the sessions to repeatedly start late and run on too long. Such things can be hard to own up to, especially when they seem like poor practice, and it would be so easy to leave out of the conversation. However, I have found that exploring what I'm most embarrassed about is *exactly* the most revealing of what is happening in the coaching relationship. We discussed in Chapter 4 how each coachee invites us to join their particular 'dance', and what seems to me my 'false steps' as a coach can be me accepting the invitation to the coachee's 'dance'. The coachee and I are, in fact, acting out what cannot yet be understood and articulated. So having the courage to 'own up' to 'mistakes' can open the door to the deepest understanding, and the possibility of transforming the coaching.

PERSONAL DEVELOPMENT

The seven-eyed model maps out the complex territory of relationships that we are involved with in coaching and supervision, territory that we have explored throughout this book. The theme is always about raising awareness, both for the coachee and the coach. In every step we take, in every aspect of the work we do, the personal development of the coach sets the bar for the depth and quality of work that is possible. This point has been understood by organisations who commission coaching:

> GSK requires coaches who are highly self-aware and actively curious about their interior world. They will have undergone significant personal development work over many years which may include therapy and/or intensive development retreats such as Hoffman or Landmark – and actively engage in regular self-reflective practices such as meditation, journaling or retreats. Such work enables coaches to be extremely clear about boundaries, giving them the ability to distinguish very clearly between what is their stuff and the coachee's. (Ridler & Co 2013, p. 6)

Peter Bluckert makes a similar point:

> Purchasers of coaching increasingly see psychological mindedness as the top-level competency they seek in executive coaches. ... [It] refers to people's *capacity to reflect upon themselves, others and the relationship between them*. It is rooted in a curiosity about how people tick and why we behave as we do. Furthermore it is about our ability to see the past in the present and make links between current issues and what has happened previously. ... There are a number of implications arising from this for the training of executive coaches as it suggests that *the personal development of the coach is every bit as important as theory and skills*. Arguably there is no meaningful distinction between personal and professional development. (2006, pp. 87–9, emphasis in original)

I hope you can see why personal development work sets the bar for what is possible, and why 'there is no meaningful distinction between personal and professional development' when working on the relational aspect of coaching. To make the point more concrete, let's focus on some of the many subjects we have addressed along the way:

- *Ask not tell*: the capacity to hold back on deeply ingrained personal/cultural patterns of intervening requires self-awareness of those patterns and the development of a different mindset which is rooted in a belief in the capability of others to find their own way forward. I'm sure you will have experienced for yourself the personal/professional challenge this poses and the shift that is needed to embed the new way of relating. From personal experience, and consistent accounts of delegates on programmes, such a change in mindset has a profound impact across a whole range of personal and professional relationships.
- **Empathy**: Goleman (1999; 2007) identifies empathy as perhaps the most fundamental human relational capacity, and it is at the heart of the coaching relationship. Empathy is a process that requires you to quieten your own thinking, planning and doing and then tune into the other person: attune to their needs; how they see the world; the conflicts they are experiencing and their hopes, ambitions and desires; and do all this without seeking to judge and change them in any way. The development of the capacity for empathy is a never-ending personal development challenge.
- *Use of self*: a capability that has been described as '*the* highest order coaching skill' (Bluckert 2006, p. 84, emphasis in original), a view with which I concur. In Chapter 4 we explored the complexity of use of self, the requirement to tune into myself in the here and now of the coaching relationship, notice and find a way of articulating that sense of self in a way that the coachee is able to hear and make use of, and then staying open to what happens next. Every aspect of 'use of self' requires a depth of self-awareness that can only come from purposeful self-reflection and familiarity with what happens in your relationship with yourself and others.
- *Difference and diversity*: self-awareness is the very essence of working effectively with difference and diversity. It is the means by which you notice your prejudices and biases which are so deep rooted that you normally just act upon them; it is the basis upon which you notice the anxiety that arises which can lead you to ignore or compulsively address difference; it is the route to engaging and 'meeting' others so we can learn and work creatively together.

We could give the same kind of account to so many of the subjects we've addressed – anxiety, mood/emotion, defences ('security operations'), transference, countertransference, parallel process, culture – and throughout all of these topics the personal and professional cannot be meaningfully separated.

It's worth noting at this point the relevance of 'emotional intelligence' to our theme of personal development. We've mentioned this concept throughout the book, a concept that has emerged in the past 20 or so years (the same kind of time-frame as coaching) and become central to activities and professions where relationships are the key consideration. There are many definitions of emotional intelligence, for example Salovey and Mayer (1990, p. 5): 'the ability to monitor one's own and others' feelings and emotions, to discriminate among them and to use this information to guide one's thinking and actions'. Or Goleman (1999, p. 317): 'Emotional intelligence is the capacity for recognising our own feelings and those of others, for motivating ourselves and for managing emotions in ourselves and in our relationships.'

Emotional intelligence has become important in coaching primarily in relation to leadership and management, for example Goleman (2003), McKee et al. (2008) and Goleman et al. (2013); indeed, developing emotional intelligence has become a key part of the coaching agenda for most people in leadership positions.

The point to notice is that the capability and skills of emotional intelligence, which are increasingly becoming central to coachees' coaching agendas, are precisely the personal capabilities and skills we need to develop as coaches if we are properly to attend to the relational aspects of coaching and to work with the coachees' emotional intelligence agendas. These skills and capacities cannot be learned from books, lectures or models. These methods have a place, but the heart of such learning is through involved engagement in forms of personal/professional practice that enable you, in a direct and emotionally involving way, to discover more about yourself and your ingrained patterns of relating to yourself and to others.

Here are some examples of the kinds of personal/professional practices we are referring to:

- *Being coached*: experience as the coachee in a coaching relationship may seem very obvious, but I've known many coaches who have never experienced this. In this role you get to be in that chair and know what it feels like to explore and become aware of things in a way that you've never experienced before. If you have a coach who works with the psychological dimension you'll have the opportunity to dig a bit deeper, connect more directly with your thinking, feeling and behaviour, and maybe begin to grasp some of your own habitual patterns of relating. You can also connect with the anxiety such exploration can evoke as you challenge existing patterns and maybe risk trying something new. To put it in stronger terms: no one should coach without having experienced the role of coachee – without having been in that chair.
- *Supervision*: we've seen that supervision is now a requirement for ethical professional practice, but more fundamentally it provides an important opportunity for reflection and paying attention to relational dynamics, both in how you manage yourself (self-regulation) and how you manage relations with others (relationship

regulation). Again I'd recommend working with a supervisor who is familiar with the psychological dimension.

- *CPD courses*: there are a whole range of courses available which can have a strong personal development element to them. If you are interested in this aspect then plan accordingly and check out whether there is a significant experiential component to the programme.

- *Reflective practice in the form of note taking and journalling*: systematic reflection is a powerful way of raising awareness, and you can structure the personal development dimension into such reflection by noticing, for example, your emotional reactions to people, your thinking, the kind of assumptions and judgements you are making, your behaviour and so on.

- *Reading relevant literature and personality tests*: there is a whole range of literature that can enhance your understanding – books on difference and diversity and on different psychological approaches, and the self-help literature on a range of subjects. You can also find out about your profile on various psychological instruments such as the Myers–Briggs Type Indicator. I have some reticence in suggesting such instruments: they can be very insightful and illuminating but at the same time a bit of a trap if too much is invested in the profile. For example, often on programmes you can hear people swopping personality profiles: 'I'm an ISFJ, what are you?' as if their personality type explains who they are and is a kind of 'fate' they are stuck with. Such profiles can be useful as a source of self-understanding when part of a wider programme of personal development, but a hindrance if taken to indicate fixed personality traits.

- *Regular personal development practices*: for example meditation and mindfulness. I also recommend you find out about Gendlin's (2003) practice of 'focusing'. His brief, straightforward 'manual' of focusing has done more to develop my practice than any other single book.

- *Personal therapy*: including therapy in this list may be rather off-putting, as therapy is usually associated with there being something 'wrong with me', and there is an understandable concern not to confuse coaching and therapy. However, many of the best coaches I know took the positive decision at some stage to have therapy, as they wanted to experience more of a 'deep-dive' into their own sense of self and how they are in relations with others. Consider it a one-to-one emotional intelligence learning lab in the service of professional development. It's not a coincidence when I say that many of the best coaches I know have taken this route; they are the ones who've had the greatest commitment to personal development and have greatly enhanced their practice as a result.

- *Experiential groups*: these are groups that are in a tradition going back to Kurt Lewin and T-groups at the National Training Laboratories in the 1940s (such groups are still run by the NTL Institute today) and the Tavistock Institute in the UK. Such groups offer a different way of learning to the usual workshop format; learning which is rooted in the immediate, here-and-now experience of the interaction between group members. Of all the forms of personal/professional development, these groups can be the most challenging and at the same time the most rewarding. All our usual ways of self and relationship management are engaged, hence the anxiety that is often present. At the same time, the possibilities for new experience and trying out new ways of relating can be transformational.

How would you recognise someone who has done the kind of personal work that is being advocated here? You're likely to notice that they:

- Listen carefully to other people.
- Attend carefully to the significance of their own thoughts and feelings in co-creating relationships.
- Empathise with and attune to other people.
- Pay attention to and work with what is happing in the here and now.
- Are comfortable staying with uncertainty and not knowing.
- Are non-defensive when challenged and keen to catch hold of their contribution to situations.
- Share with others, in an appropriate way, their experience in the moment.
- Have a sense of their 'presence' and the differing 'presences' that situations require, and, crucially, have an awareness of the impact of their presence on others.
- Have an awareness of their strengths and ingrained patterns of behaviour, and seek to take these into account in relations with others.
- Take a stand on what matters to them, whilst staying open to the views of others.

These are some of the attributes of people who have and are engaged in personal development work. A familiar and difficult situation is where people believe they have done such work because they've undertaken an academic psychological education, or been professionally involved in administering tests, or read a lot about psychology and know a lot of the theory, models and techniques, but have not been experientially involved in the work. As a commissioner of coaching observed:

> Of all the aspects to judge, self-awareness is the hardest. Where there is limited awareness it is easy – people talk of going on courses or learning skills or just own that they haven't really done much here. It becomes trickier when a coach is aware of what personal development work comprises and therefore is skilled in the language but not really done the work. This, to coin a Buddhist phrase, 'near enemy' is the most difficult coach to assess properly. They may harbour deep seated issues which are hidden in their public face. (Ridler & Co 2013, p. 6)

Personal development work is vital in developing your professional coaching capability. It is always a joy for me, at the end of coaching programmes, to look round the room and hear about people's personal journeys, and to know what they are saying is true because I too (and everyone else in the room) have seen those journeys take place. There is usually a taken-for-granted acceptance that having completed the programme they are now able to coach: the unexpected outcome – which people often see as more profound for their lives in general, and their coaching in particular – is the personal transformation. It is this transformation that gives them the belief in the possibilities of coaching to transform lives – because they've been on (and are on) that same journey.

IMPLICATIONS FOR PRACTICE

Take some time to review your supervision arrangements:

- Do you have a supervisor, and if so how often do you meet?
- Is the supervision meeting your needs?
- Review your supervision against the bullet points in the section 'Having begun supervision' and maybe identify some ways you can develop the supervision relationship.

Review your attitude to and involvement with the personal development aspect of your progress as a coach:

- What do you make of the proposition that personal and professional development are two sides of the same coin, and that personal development is vital for you as a coach?
- Are you engaged in any personal development activities that are enhancing your capability as a coach?
- How would you rate yourself on the personal development work you've done, in relation to the questions above?

RECOMMENDED READING

On supervision, Hawkins and Smith (2013) *Coaching, Mentoring and Organisational Consultancy* and Hawkins and Shohet (2012) *Supervision in the Helping Professions* are good places to start. I also recommend de Haan (2012) *Supervision in Action: A Relational Approach to Coaching and Consulting Supervision*.

It's somewhat difficult to suggest reading for the personal development aspects, as this is primarily something to get involved with rather than read about. Nevertheless, I think the Goleman books on emotional intelligence are a good source – (1999) *Working with Emotional Intelligence*; (2003) *The New Leaders*; (2007) *Social Intelligence* – as they lay out the case for personal development and provide a framework for the kind of personal and interpersonal 'competencies' that are required.

9

Coaching Relationship in Practice: The Evidence Base

As its title suggests, this book puts relationship at the heart of the coaching process. We have discussed some models and skills, but they have not been the main focus. It is reasonable to ask, therefore, about the evidence base for this approach: is there any research that supports the proposition, which is explicit and implicit throughout the book, that the relationship is fundamental to effective practice? It is the evidence for this proposition that we'll address in this chapter. We'll also touch on the whole subject of 'evidence-based practice' because the research cannot properly be understood without this context and, though the subject may sound somewhat unexciting, it is the source of strong passions and has the potential to transform the whole field of coaching in the way it has transformed counselling and psychotherapy.

What is your attitude and practice in relation to research and evidence?

- Do you think it is important to engage in research?
- Have you explored the evidence base for your own practice?
- Have you come across the notion of 'evidence-based practice' and if so what have you made of it?
- Do you know the literature – books/journals – on research in coaching?

It's fair to say that research into the effectiveness of coaching is still in its early stages (Passmore and Fillery-Travis 2011). De Haan et al. estimate that 'There are probably fewer than 20 robust quantitative outcome studies throughout the entire coaching literature ... and as yet no rigorous randomised controlled trial studies' (2013, pp. 2–3). Given this situation de Haan and others have turned to research in psychotherapy, a discipline which is a 'close cousin' to coaching, with decades of research into the same subject: 'As McKenna and Davis (2009) argue, the coaching field can learn from the fact that in the older and more established profession of psychotherapy, the same question of effectiveness has been rigorously studied since at least the 1930s' (ibid., p. 3). This turn to psychotherapy is also particularly apt as many of the current approaches to coaching are explicitly based on therapeutic models, as the contents page of any handbook on coaching will quickly show (e.g. Cox et al. 2014).

What can we learn, then, from the research in counselling and psychotherapy? The first thing to note is that research is a fiercely contested field. Every significant finding is challenged and subject to varying interpretations, depending upon the orientations of those involved. This is particularly so around research into the comparative effectiveness of different approaches, for example comparisons between cognitive behavioural, psychodynamic, existential and what has come to be called the 'common factors' approach (of which more below). The research is so fiercely contested because there is so much at stake – passionate belief and allegiance to particular approaches, reputations, livelihoods, jobs and access to funding that is the life-blood of any profession. To understand why it is that so much is at stake we need to look briefly at the notion of evidence-based practice.

The evidence-based practice movement, which began primarily in health care (Rowland and Goss 2000), is rooted in the entirely reasonable belief that if very large sums of money are being spent on treatments (primarily by governments and insurance companies) then we need rigorous research to show 'what works for whom' (Fonagy et al. 2005) in the most effective and cost-efficient way. In the UK, NICE (National Institute for Health and Care Excellence) is the body that rules on what treatments are supported by the evidence, and millions of pounds of investment by, for example, pharmaceutical companies, is at stake in the judgements it makes. The same kinds of questions confront the purchasers of coaching, namely 'What is the return on investment of coaching?', and it's likely that they'll increasingly be looking at the evidence base of the approaches offered by providers of coaching in making their decisions. So what might seem like somewhat academic research pursuits have direct implications for the 'bottom line', for both purchasers and providers of coaching.

The question of what is the most cost-effective therapeutic approach has, for many people, one clear answer: it is cognitive behavioural therapy (CBT), as this is the approach that is best supported by research evidence and hence most often designated the treatment of choice. This 'result' is profoundly transforming the counselling and psychotherapy profession in the UK, as the NHS is now the main provider of 'talking therapies', and its funding decisions are shaping the nature of services that are provided, the kind of training that is supported and the professional opportunities for counsellors, therapists and other practitioners involved in the delivery of services – and it is CBT that is favoured in all these areas.

This picture of a clear 'winner' becomes, however, a bit cloudier if we dig deeper into the research process. It has repeatedly been pointed out (Cooper 2008; Wampold and Imel 2001) that the 'gold standard' of research, randomised control trials (RCTs), favour approaches that are structured, time limited, goal focused and based upon a manual. CBT is exactly that kind of approach, and this has enabled it to generate large amounts of research evidence demonstrating its efficacy. On the other hand, these self-same requirements for setting up RCTs are anathema to the likes of person-centred or existential practitioners and pose considerable difficulties for psychodynamic therapies. It is inconceivable, for example, that the person-centred approach could be inscribed in a manual, as this would undermine the fundamental philosophy of the approach. Consequently, there is an absence of the required 'gold standard' research on such approaches. This situation casts a new light on the statement that CBT is the approach that is best supported by the evidence, a statement that can easily be mistaken to mean that CBT is the 'best' and most effective treatment. The statement actually means no more than it says: CBT is the approach where we have the most evidence of a particular kind (RCTs), not that it is better than the other approaches where we lack such evidence. In this sense, the predominance of CBT is, in large measure, an artefact of the research process.

Much of the research on efficacy has compared the outcomes of patients receiving treatment with control groups who did not receive the treatment (for example, patients on a waiting list). In studies where the effectiveness of different approaches has been directly compared – where the approaches have gone 'head to head' – the picture of a clear 'winner' becomes more cloudy. In such research one of the best-established findings is that 'There is an overwhelming body of evidence to suggest that there is little difference in how efficacious different therapies are' (Cooper 2008, p. 50).

So when different approaches are directly compared there is no clear winner. And the initially clear picture of the best-supported approach becomes foggier still when allegiance effects are taken into account. Allegiance effects are the tendency for researchers to find and report evidence that supports their own orientation. Such an effect can be understood in terms of 'experimenter expectancy', which is mostly outside of the researchers' awareness and can show up in even the most rigorously controlled 'double-blind' experimental designs (ibid., p. 49). In a major study (Luborsky et al. 1999) found that over two-thirds of the variance in outcomes could be attributed to allegiance effects and that 'there are no articles in the entire literature published by a first author who is the founder of a treatment, where the results are counter to the author's allegiance' (ibid., p. 102). Westen et al. (2004) found that in more than nine out of ten cases they could predict the outcome of a comparative study simply on the basis of the researchers' allegiance. In other words, in all the published research, across the board, the allegiance of the researchers has a powerful impact on the outcome of studies, studies which are at the same time the basis for judgements about the efficacy of different approaches.

Consider your experience of different coaching methods:

- Do you have allegiance to a particular approach or approaches to coaching?
- If you do, how do you think this affects the kind of literature you read and your evaluation of the value of other approaches?
- In coaching, or any other field (e.g. politics) have you ever read anything that led you to changing your mind on a significant issue?

In light of the above, research on the differential effectiveness of approaches has famously been characterised in terms of the verdict of the dodo bird in *Alice in Wonderland* who, when judging a race, declared that 'Everyone has won and all must have prizes' (Luborsky et al. 1975).

Though there is no 'winner' in terms of identifying particular approaches or techniques, there is at the same time overwhelming evidence to show that psychotherapy is effective (Lambert and Ogles 2004). This raises the question, if improvements cannot be attributed to theory, skills and techniques of any particular approach, what else can be responsible for the positive outcomes? The answer given by many is that there are **common factors** shared by all approaches that are responsible for the improvements, common factors that are primarily relational in nature. A well-known formulation of this approach is 'Lambert's pie', a chart approximately summarising research on the contribution of different factors to outcomes of therapy (Asay and Lambert, 1999):

1. Coachee variables and extra therapeutic events: 40 per cent.
2. Therapeutic relationship: 30 per cent.
3. Techniques and models: 15 per cent.
4. Expectancy and placebo effects: 15 per cent.

You'll see that this formulation does attribute some efficacy to techniques and models. At the same time three of the four categories (1, 2 and 4) are relational in nature, contributing, in this estimation, 85 per cent of the improvement in coachees.

The research on common factors is vast (Hubble et al. 1999). Rather than go into detail I'll draw out some of the findings that are particularly important and their direct relevance for us as practising coaches. I'll not reference all the studies as I summarise the various findings, but if you are interested in the sources you'll find them in Cooper (2008), Chapters 4 to 7.

1. COACHEE VARIABLES AND EXTRA THERAPEUTIC EVENTS

You'll see that Lambert attributes most significance to the client and extra therapeutic events: it is the **client** rather than the **practitioner** who is the 'hero' in the story. This is important to grasp, because so often in the coaching literature and education/training the focus is on what the coach 'does' to the coachee, a scenario that frames the coachee as a somewhat passive recipient of the coach's ministrations: for example, their use of a particular model, technique or skill. Paying attention to the research evidence helps us refocus our attention on the coachee, what she brings to the relationship and what will enable her to get the most out of coaching.

Perhaps the most important factor of all for success is the attitude, motivation and involvement of the coachee in the process, and a key factor in this is whether the coachee has freely chosen to engage in coaching and whether they are actively involved in the work. This may seem obvious, but it is worth remembering as there are many situations where coachees may not have freely chosen the coaching, perhaps because they think it is politic to 'go along' with the offer, or more subtly because coaching is part of a 'package', such as a leadership development programme, and has not been an explicit choice. The research would suggest that checking coachee motivation to ensure that there is real 'buy-in' is of paramount importance at the beginning, and that there is a sense of active collaboration throughout the work.

Along with motivation, the coachee's confidence in the process, based on a realistic expectation of what will happen, has a significant impact on outcomes. Again, this chimes with our discussions of proper contracting, but perhaps it underlines more clearly the importance of 'educating' the coachee about coaching and what is involved, and taking time to set up expectations of the different roles. It is also important for the coach to tailor the work to the particular needs of the coachee, for example how they are positioned in terms of the stages of change. Prochaska et al. (1998) have convincingly demonstrated that coachees need different things at different stages of change, and it is important for the coach to recognise this and work accordingly.

Under the heading of 'coachee variables' Lambert includes 'extra therapeutic events', i.e. other things in the life of the coachee that may affect the work. In terms of coaching, one vital aspect of this is the level of personal and professional support – or, to use the gestalt expression, the 'environmental support' – available to the coachee which will enable and sustain change. This may again seem like an obvious point, but the significance of such support can easily be missed if attention is focused on the coach and what they do. Also, many of our coachees, particularly those in commercial organisations focused on performance, are not very good at asking for support or drawing upon the support that is available. They are quite likely to be very self-sufficient and view seeking support as 'asking for help' and thus a sign of weakness. The research, then, is invaluable in holding our attention on what can so easily be overlooked: the 'environmental support' for change.

2. THERAPEUTIC RELATIONSHIP

The relationship aspect focuses on how the coach and coachee get on with each other, what they co-create and what happens between them. The kinds of things clients say about what they found helpful in therapy is worthy of note:

> From a client perspective, the most important aspects of therapy typically are the 'non-technological factors': having a time and place to talk; having someone care, listen and understand; having someone provide encouragement and reassurance; and having someone offer an external perspective and advice. (Bohart and Tallman 1991, p. 51)

Alongside the research on general aspects of the coaching relationship, there has been considerable research on specific aspects of particular importance for coaching:

- *The working alliance*. The concept originated in psychoanalytic therapies and refers to the conscious, adult-to-adult aspects of the relationship, through which agreement is reached about the goals, tasks and purposes of coaching, and the degree to which these pragmatic aspects are set within a relationship of positive regard, acceptance and trust. The concept was developed in contrast to the transferential aspects of relationships, where strong emotion and confusion can reign, and where reality can get somewhat 'lost'. It is the working alliance that can keep the work on track even through difficult times.

  The research suggests that establishing a strong working alliance is key to the success of the relationship (see also de Haan and Duckworth 2012). If we unpack the concept we find that we are again on familiar ground, with clear contracting and, as discussed earlier in relation to the coachee, addressing coachee motivation and their understanding of the process. It also underlines the importance of attending to the dynamics of the relationship, particularly if there is discontent or a drop in motivation, as the coachee may not explicitly acknowledge these and they can lead to missed sessions, lack of involvement in the process and the early termination of the coaching.
- *Empathy*. This is a quality that has been central throughout the book, and the research findings support the belief that it is a vital aspect of the coaching relationship. Some research shows it to be more important than any particular techniques and maybe even more important than the therapeutic alliance, though clearly it is always interwoven with that alliance. When asked about what has been most important in their therapy, empathy has often been rated highly. It has also been identified as an important aspect of approaches such as CBT where the qualities of the relationship are not the focus of the approach.
- *Use of self*. Throughout the book we have argued that use of self is the highest-level coaching capability. Is there any evidence to support this claim? Unfortunately

the concept itself does not figure in quantitative research findings on outcomes that we are reviewing, though there is research on related concepts such as congruence and self-disclosure, and we can draw together some of the research around these two ideas.

In relation to congruence, defined in terms of genuineness and interpersonal honesty, the research findings are ambivalent, with only about one-third of studies showing a positive relation between congruence and outcomes.

In relation to self-disclosure, the research literature has a useful distinction between 'self-disclosure' and 'self-involving statements'. Self-disclosure is practitioners' disclosures of aspects of their own lives, maybe sharing their own experience of something the coachee is discussing. Self-involving statements, sometimes called 'immediacy', are practitioners' personal responses in the here and now (e.g. 'I felt excited when you said that'), and it seems to me this is the closest approximation there is to use of self. There seems to be more research on self-disclosure than self-involving statements, and this research generally indicates a positive relation between such disclosure and outcomes. Judicious and moderate amounts of disclosure are related to a positive view of the practitioner and enhance the quality of the relationship; they are sometimes reported to be the most helpful of all interventions. Where self-involving and self-disclosing interventions have been compared, some research indicates that self-involving statements are seen as more expert and trustworthy, though positive self-involving statements are regarded more favourably than negative self-involving statements.

It is apparent, therefore, that the claim that use of self, per se, is the highest-level coaching skill has not yet been researched in any depth, perhaps in part because of the difficulty of defining it. At the same time there is some support for the two forms of disclosure.

3. TECHNIQUES AND MODELS

What of some of the skills we've been advocating in this book: is there relevant research? There is considerable research to show that listening is highly valued by coachees. Similarly there is a positive view of paraphrasing.

A constant theme throughout the book has been the importance of deepening awareness and engaging emotionally. There is considerable evidence to support the importance of the arousal and expression of emotion, though it is important to note that 'catharsis' per se, i.e. the simple experiencing/expression of emotion, is insufficient; it also needs to be meaningful. This aligns with the understanding throughout the book that meaning and emotion are always intertwined, and with the process we described of attending to emotion and finding words or symbols that resonate with and catch the meaning of the emotion.

There is evidence to support gestalt two-chair and empty-chair as techniques for raising and deepening awareness, as a 'potent form of intervention' (Orlinsky et al. 2004, p. 323). Gendlin's 'focusing' is also supported by research as a way of deepening experience.

4. EXPECTANCY AND PLACEBO EFFECTS

I find this one of the most intriguing areas as it gathers together some of the least tangible but vital aspects of the coaching relationship. It takes us into the territory of self-fulfilling prophecies, as captured in the quote from Henry Ford: 'Whether you think you can, or you think you can't – you're right', where belief, motivation, action and outcome are all interwoven. It also take us to the origins of the 'common factors' approach in therapy, to the influential book written by Jerome Frank in 1961, *Persuasion and Healing* (Frank and Frank 1993), which places therapy in a long tradition of forms of healing where the various ailments afflicting people are understood as forms of 'demoralisation', and the many different 'therapies', in all their different forms (religious and secular) with all their different theories and techniques, are in essence doing one thing: combatting demoralisation by instilling **hope** (Snyder et al. 1999; Scovern 1999). I find Frank's approach particularly intriguing in relation to our earlier discussion of mood and emotion in the coaching relationship.

The power and significance of such complexes of meaning and motivation become most apparent in the notion of 'placebo', where there are many extraordinary accounts of the impact of belief on medical conditions, some of which are long-standing and apparently intractable (Moerman 2002). The reality of placebo effects are now recognised as so important that they have to be taken into account in research, where forms of treatment have to demonstrate that they are more effective than a placebo alone. Indeed, in medicine in general, and psychotherapy in particular, it is often found that the placebo is as, or more, effective than the treatment being tested. That such an experimental procedure is required, even before the ensuing results are considered, shows that there is something very powerful at work – something most people are unaware of to do with expectation and motivation that is highly significant.

These findings are as relevant to coaching as they are to therapy and medicine, and it is important to note that we are not just talking about the motivation/expectations of coachees; the 'morale' of the coach is equally important, as was evident in the earlier discussion of 'allegiance effects'. The power of the expectations of practitioners was dramatically shown by Rosenthal and Jacobson (1968) in their seminal study *Pygmalion in the Classroom: Teacher Expectation and Pupils' Intellectual Development*, in which they showed that teachers' beliefs and expectations about children significantly affect the subsequent IQ scores of pupils. Likewise for us as coaches, the

'Pygmalion effect', or self-fulfilling prophecies, are in play; the beliefs we have about ourselves – our self-confidence – and the beliefs we have about our coachees, will undoubtedly have a significant impact on the outcomes of our work.

Overall then, there is considerable evidence to support the position that 'common factors' are important in coaching, factors that are relational in nature. One caveat is required: researchers who are advocates of the 'common factors' approach are no less susceptible to alliance effects than researchers who believe in particular approaches. In research, as in every other aspect of life, there is no 'view from nowhere' – how we are positioned always has an impact.

IN SUMMARY, WHAT DOES THE EVIDENCE SAY?

How can we summarise the complex and often controversial evidence for the effectiveness of different approaches in therapy (and by implication, in coaching too)? Cooper, after laying out in detail the evidence and various arguments, draws it all together thus:

> at the heart of most successful therapies is a coachee who is willing and able to become involved in making changes to her or his life. If that coachee then encounters a therapist who she or he trusts, likes and feels able to collaborate with, the coachee can make use of a wide range of techniques and practices to move toward her or his goals. ... The evidence suggests that the key predictor of outcome remains the extent to which the coachee is willing and able to make use of whatever the therapist provides. (2008, p. 157)

Quite so, and this tallies with my own experience in coaching.

Consider your coaching methods:

- What are your favourite skills and techniques?
- Have you ever checked the research literature to see if there is any evidence on the effectiveness of those skills and techniques?
- Have you ever based your practice on what you've discovered in the research literature?

REFLECTIONS ON EVIDENCE AND EVIDENCE-BASED PRACTICE

It seems to me that it is vital that we take note of and draw on research to inform our practice; to have a 'research-informed mindset'. Such a mindset can provide an important challenge to our beliefs and practices, and also raise awareness of new possibilities in our work. To give an example of what I mean, recent research on feedback on client progress in therapy has shown that noticing and addressing poor client 'progress' in the early stages of the relationship can significantly reduce dropout rates and improve outcomes (Cooper 2008, pp. 151–2). Such research is food for thought about my own practice, raising awareness of the issue and suggestive of how I might improve what I do.

At the same time as fully supporting the use of evidence to inform our practice, I notice anxiety and resistance in me to claims that coaching should be 'evidenced-based' if this means more than being 'research-informed; if this means that evidence is to be *the* primary reference point and guide to practice. There is one very practical reason for such reticence: as the discussion in this chapter demonstrates, evidence does not provide the requisite firm ground – the evidence base is a highly contested field that is awash with allegiance effects.

There is another less obvious but I believe powerful reason for my reticence, which, for me, goes back a long way to my PhD about the philosophy of the behavioural sciences. It became apparent to me that claims to being 'scientific' were often claims to some kind of superiority over other – usually rival – approaches; claims, you could say, about 'market share'. 'Evidence-based practice' can be, I believe, the contemporary equivalent of the claim to 'being scientific' (you can check for yourself how often the terms 'evidence-based' and 'scientific' appear alongside each other in publications), and my concern is that some of the same dynamics can apply: i.e. 'Our approach is scientific, evidence-based and thereby superior to other approaches.'

It is a powerful claim of course, and one that is hard to challenge; who could argue against the proposition that our practice should be evidenced-based? And at the same time I have no doubt that these self-same dynamics are at play in the claims and counter-claims for the effectiveness of differing forms of therapy – how could they not be when there is so much at stake? And the stakes are similarly high in coaching. The 'antidote' to the influence of such claims, and the way forward to the appropriate use of evidence, is to engage properly with research and the research literature – to understand, for example, the basics of the research process and terminology (for example, RCTs, 'effect size', 'meta-analysis') – to give yourself the best chance of making informed judgements about the validity and reliability of research and give evidence its proper place in your practice.

I'd also like to flag up an issue that goes deeper still, and is one of the reasons why exploring the whole notion of evidence-based practice can be both fascinating and essential if you want to grasp the foundations of practice. The issue is that research does not just collect evidence about a subject: the way we go about the research plays an active part in constructing what we then 'find'; we cannot 'measure something' without changing it. This is why I said at the beginning of the chapter that evidence-based practice has the capacity to transform the very thing it researches.

Let me give one obvious but very powerful example from the world of counselling and psychotherapy. As stated earlier, the 'gold standard' of research is the RCT, a method taken from medical research, and so, unsurprisingly, the medical model underlies such an approach, where research involves investigating the effects of particular treatments on particular illnesses. Such a model requires a distinct, replicable form of treatment and a distinct identifiable medical condition. Taking evidence-based practice into therapy has necessarily meant importing the medical model into therapy (Wampold and Imel 2001), such that therapy is now increasingly viewed as a branch of medicine where therapists treat distinct medical conditions as defined in classifications of mental illness (such as the *Diagnostic and Statistical Manual of Mental Disorders*, APA 2013). Just as research in medicine asks about the dose of treatment required for a particular illness, so research in therapy enquires about the dose of therapy required (e.g. the number of sessions of CBT needed to treat depression). You can see that this view of therapy is a far cry from what many therapists thought they were about – helping people with 'problems in living', for example, with relationships, purpose and meaning in life, mourning, self-confidence and so forth.

How will the move towards evidence-based practice play out in coaching? Will coaching be transformed in ways analogous to the changes in therapy? Only time will tell, though I am anxious, as trends and themes that are familiar to me from therapy seem to be emerging in coaching. I recommend you keep a sharp eye on what you think is at the heart of coaching, and use this as a compass to guide you through the shifting definitions and practices that you are likely to encounter.

IMPLICATIONS FOR PRACTICE

It may be that questions of research and evidence have not been addressed on the coaching programmes you've been on, so this chapter might be food for thought and an opportunity to reflect on the evidence base of your own practice. I invite you to consider the following:

- What is your overall attitude and interest in research and evidence?
- Do you have a 'researched-informed mindset'?
- Do you know where to go to find the research/evidence?
- Are you interested in doing research, perhaps into your own practice, and if so how would you go about it?
- What do you make of the proposition that we inevitably change whatever we research?
- What do you make of the position I've outlined about the significance of evidence-based practice and its possible implications for coaching?

RECOMMENDED READING

The literature on research is extensive, complex and often technical. If you want a succinct, thoughtful and very readable account of key issues, debates, controversies and findings in counselling and psychotherapy I strongly recommend Cooper (2008) *Essential Research Findings in Counselling and Psychotherapy.*

There are a number of other books which give more detailed accounts of the history, issues and debates on research and evidence-based practice in psychotherapy and medicine which will give you an invaluable context for making sense of current debates. If you would like to follow this up I suggest you have a look at Wampold and Imel (2001) *The Great Psychotherapy Debate*, Duncan et al. (2009) *The Heart and Soul of Change: Delivering What Works in Therapy*, and Norcross et al. (2006) *Evidence-Based Practices in Mental Health*.

Frank and Frank (1993) *Persuasion and Healing: A Comparative Study of Psychotherapy* is a great book if you'd like to have your thinking widened and challenged about what is involved in the 'healing process' in its widest sense, and coaching would certainly be included in that tradition.

The 'power of placebo' is one of the least-known stories, though it is an extraordinary phenomenon with important implications for coaching. If you'd like to know more I recommend Daniel Moerman (2002) *Meaning, Medicine and the 'Placebo Effect'.*

Conclusion: Putting Your Signature on It

Having observed and worked with hundreds of coaches, one thing is obvious – each person coaches in their own way; each person has their own 'style' of coaching. This is no different to every other aspect of life, whether as a parent, manager, teacher, driver or footballer; we all have our own particular way of doing things. There is a 'craft' to learn in becoming a coach, as there is in any professional practice, and with that a desire and anxiety to do it right; do it, you might say, 'by the book'. At the same time it's important to recognise the obvious: that each of us 'puts our own signature' on the work; each of us develops our own distinctive way of coaching. And given that the coaching relationship is a co-creation, I'm sure you can see the importance of this signature – woven, as it is, into the very fabric and tapestry of each relationship.

Our signature is the gathering-up of the strands of our lives into a particular 'way of being' – a 'presence', a distinctive, recognisable 'style' that we bring to every activity, coaching included. I think of this signature in terms of *Stimmung*: our attunement to the world. There are many different approaches to coaching, as is evidenced in its many and varied definitions, and in the burgeoning literature on the subject. As with the analogy of the radio, each of us is attuned to certain 'stations', to a particular way of going about coaching (tuned perhaps to attend to performance, to models and techniques, or to relationships), and as we tune into one station we tune out of others. Each of us resonates to certain traditions across the broad spectrum of coaching, and develops our signature presence accordingly.

Consider your attunement to the world:

- What do you make of the idea that we each have our own distinctive style, a 'signature' presence?
- What awareness do you have of your own signature? Can you see it 'written' into your everyday relationships and activities, and into your coaching?
- What are the strands of your life that contribute to this signature?
- Are you attuned to particular approaches to coaching which you draw upon to fashion your style?

I'd like to 'sign off' this book by saying some more about my own signature, partly to enable you to situate what I've written in relation to the various approaches and traditions of coaching; partly as an example of the way attunement is woven into the fabric of the coaching relationship; but mostly because I have an intimation that it is our own attunement and its resonance with coachees that brings life, creativity and energy to the work.

I said two things in the Introduction that are clues to my *Stimmung*: first, I talked about questions of the meaning and purpose of life that have always haunted me; and second, I mentioned that in recent years existential approaches are the ones which have had the most profound influence on my coaching. I'm sure you can see the link! Existentialism poses questions about the meaning and purpose of life: about what matters, what makes life worthwhile and how to take 'ownership' of life, particularly when to do so challenges the accepted cultural taken-for-granted ways of doing things. Though acknowledging the past and the present, it is an approach that is future focused. It is concerned with the possibilities of what we can *be*; of what we can make our lives ('Higher than actuality stands **possibility**', Heidegger 1962, p. 63, emphasis in original).

I realise I attune to these existential aspects of the coachee's story – I am drawn to them and respond to them without deliberate thought or intention – and it is when they 'strike a chord' with the coachee that we engage in the most intense and fulfilling work. I find myself asking questions like 'What matters most to you in this?' or 'What makes this work meaningful to do?', and the replies can go right to the heart of the issues and result in very feelingful and transformative conversations. And it is these conversations that bring direction, energy and commitment when addressing the 'there' of 'what got you here won't get you there' because, as we've seen, getting to 'there' often involves daunting personal and professional challenges which must really matter for the coachee to genuinely commit to change. It can involve (to use some of the existential language which I love) taking a 'stand on our being': i.e. standing up for what I think is right though others may strongly disagree and disapprove – which of course can be the essence of true leadership.

A word that catches the essence of this approach is 'authenticity', and you can no doubt see how this notion has been implicit throughout the book: for example, in 'use of self', and the constant refrain that the personal and professional are always interwoven. A danger with notions of authenticity is that they can prioritise 'me' over others: 'It's what I want and my purpose that become paramount.' A deeper understanding of authenticity is 'true to self and true to others' (Guignon 2004; Taylor 1992). It is this spirit, I hope, that has been present throughout the book, for instance in the discussion of managing complex relationships, trust and even-handedness in relations with coachees and organisations.

There is, of course, the other side of the coin: by tuning into the existential themes I'm likely to tune out, be more challenged by, or work less well with coachees who are differently attuned; who may, for example, be looking for something that directly addresses more pragmatic, performance-focused business results. 'True to self and true to others' reappears, this time in questions of how to work ethically and properly with people who want something that does not resonate with my approach. These are questions that I continue to work with.

So what are the implications of this for your practice?

- What is it that brings coaching most 'alive' for you?
- In what ways do you invite coachees on to your favourite 'ground'?
- Can you be 'true to self and true to others' both in developing as a coach and working with coachees? Can you be open to difference and diversity whilst retaining a strong sense of your own path?

The metaphor and images of path and journey really capture for me the essence of coaching: both learning about it and working with coachees. It's a metaphor that also seems right for this book, as I have a distinct sense of being in a different place with you now compared to where we were at the beginning; and I too have been changed in the writing.

I wish you well on your journey knowing full well, based on experience, that for most of you it will be a transformational journey – something I'm guessing you already know.

RECOMMENDED READING

Graham Lee (2003) *Leadership Coaching: From Personal Insight to Organisational Excellence* brings together the themes of authentic leadership and working with ingrained patterns of behaviour in a way that concretely illustrates the idea in this and previous chapters.

Charles Guignon (2004) *Being Authentic* and Charles Taylor (1992) *The Ethics of Authenticity* consider authenticity with a depth and rigour that is vital to grasping properly the complexity and richness of the concept.

References

APA (2013) *Diagnostic and Statistical Manual of Mental Disorders, Fifth Edition* (*DSM-5*). Arlington, VA: American Psychiatric Association.

Asay, T. and Lambert, M. (1999) 'The empirical case for the common factors in therapy: quantitative findings', in M. Hubble, B. Duncan and S. Miller (eds), *The Heart and Soul of Change: What Works in Therapy*. Washington, DC: American Psychological Association.

Baldwin, M. (2000) *The Use of Self in Therapy*. Binghamton, NY: Haworth Press.

Barton Evans, F. (1996) *Harry Stack Sullivan: Interpersonal Theory and Psychotherapy*. London: Routledge.

Beebe, B. and Lachmann, F. (2002) *Infant Research and Adult Treatment: Co-constructing Interactions*. Hillsdale, NJ: The Analytic Press.

Blattner, W. (2006) *Heidegger's Being and Time: A Reader's Guide*. London: Continuum.

Bluckert, P. (2006) *Psychological Dimension of Executive Coaching*. Maidenhead: Open University Press.

Bohart, A. and Tallman, K. (1991) *How Coachees Make Therapy Work: The Process of Active Self-Healing*. Washington, DC: American Psychological Association.

Bowlby, J. (2005) *A Secure Base*. Abingdon: Routledge.

Brunning, H. (ed.) (2006) *Executive Coaching: Systems-Psychodynamic Perspective*. London: Karnac.

Clarkson, P. with Cavicchia, S. (2013) *Gestalt Counselling in Action* (4th edn). London: Sage.

Clarkson, P. and Mackewn, J. (1993) *Fritz Perls*. London: Sage.

Clutterbuck, D. and Megginson, D. (2013) *Beyond Goals: Effective Strategies for Coaching and Mentoring*. Farnham: Gower.

Cooper, M. (2008) *Essential Research Findings in Counselling and Psychotherapy: The Facts Are Friendly*. London: Sage (in association with BACP).

Cox, E., Bachkirova, T. and Clutterbuck, D. (eds) (2014) *The Complete Handbook of Coaching* (2nd edn). London: Sage.

De Haan, E. (2008) *Relational Coaching: Journeys Towards Mastering One-to-One Learning*. Chichester: John Wiley and Sons.

De Haan, E. (2012) *Supervision in Action: A Relational Approach to Coaching and Consulting Supervision*. Maidenhead: Open University Press.

De Haan, E. and Duckworth, A. (2012) 'The coaching relationship and other "common factors" in executive coaching outcome', in E. De Haan and C. Sills (eds), *Coaching Relationships: The Relational Coaching Fieldbook*. Faringdon: Libri.

De Haan, E. and Sills, C. (eds) (2012) *Coaching Relationships: The Relational Coaching Fieldbook*. Farington: Libri.

De Haan, E., Duckworth, A., Birch, B. and Jones, C. (2013) 'Executive coaching outcome research: the contributions of common factors such as relationship, personality match and self-efficacy', *Consulting Psychology Journal: Practice and Research*, 65(1): 40–57.

DeYoung, P. (2003) *Relational Psychotherapy: A Primer*. New York: Brunner-Routledge.

Duncan, B., Miller, S., Wampold, B. and Hubble, M. (2009) *The Heart and Soul of Change: Delivering What Works in Therapy*. Washington, DC: American Psychological Association.

Dylan, B. (1965) *Ballad of a Thin Man*. Warner Bros. Inc.; renewed 1993 by Special Rider Music.

European Mentoring and Coaching Council (2008) *Code of Ethics*. Available at: www.emccouncil.org/src/ultimo/models/Download/4.pdf (accessed April 2015).

Fonagy, P., Target, M., Cottrell, D. and Phillips, J. (2005) *What Works for Whom? A Critical Review of Treatments for Children and Adolescents*. New York: Guilford Press.

Frank, J. and Frank, J. (1993) *Persuasion and Healing: A Comparative Study of Psychotherapy*. Baltimore, MD: Johns Hopkins University Press.

Freud, S. ([1910] 2001) 'The future prospects of psychoanalytic therapy', in J. Strachey (ed.), *The Standard Edition of the Complete Psychological Works of Sigmund Freud* (vol. 11). London: Hogarth Press.

Freud, S. ([1912] 1978) 'The dynamics of transference', in J. Strachey (ed.), *The Standard Edition of the Complete Psychological Works of Sigmund Freud* (vol. 12). London: Hogarth Press.

Freud, S. (2003) *An Outline of Psychoanalysis*. London: Penguin Modern Classics.

Freud, S. (2010) *An Outline of Psycho-Analysis*. Eastford, CT: Martino Fine Books.

Frost, S. (2014) *The Inclusion Imperative: How Real Business Inclusion Creates Better Business and Builds Better Societies*. London: Kogan Page.

Gallwey, W.T. (1986) *The Inner Game of Tennis*. London: Pan Books.

Gallwey, W.T. (2007) *The Inner Game of Work*. New York: Random House.

Gendlin, E. (1978–9) 'Befindlichkeit: Heidegger and the philosophy of psychology', *Review of Existential Psychology & Psychiatry: Heidegger and Psychology*, 16(1–3): 43–71. Available at www.focusing.org/gendlin_befindlichkeit.html (accessed March 2015).

Gendlin, E. (2003) *Focusing: How to Gain Direct Access to Your Body's Knowledge: How to Open Up Your Deeper Feelings and Intuition*. London: Rider.

Goldsmith, M. (2012) *What Got You Here Won't Get You There: How Successful People Become Even More Successful*. London: Profile Books.

Goleman, D. (1999) *Working with Emotional Intelligence*. London: Bloomsbury.

Goleman, D. (2003) *The New Leaders: Transforming the Art of Leadership*. London: Sphere.

Goleman, D. (2007) *Social Intelligence: The New Science of Human Relationships*. London: Arrow.

Goleman, D., Boyatzis, R. and McKee, A. (2001) 'Primal leadership: the hidden driver of great performance', *Harvard Business Review*, 79(11): 42–51.

Goleman, D., Boyatzis, R. and McKee, A. (2013) *Primal Leadership: Unleashing the Power of Emotional Intelligence*. Boston, MA: Harvard Business Review Press.

Gomez, L. (1997) *An Introduction to Object Relations*. London: Free Association Press.

Grant, A.M. (2012) 'An integrated model of goal-focused coaching: an evidence-based framework for teaching and practice', *International Coaching Psychology Review*, 7(2): 146–65.

Grant, A.M. (2014) 'Autonomy support, relationship satisfaction and goal focus in the coach–coachee relationship: which best predicts coaching success?', *Coaching: An International Journal of Theory, Research and Practice*, 7(1): 18–38.

Gray, A. (1994) *An Introduction to the Therapeutic Frame.* London: Routledge.

Guignon, C. (2004) *Being Authentic.* London: Routledge.

Harris, T.A. (2012) *I'm OK – You're OK*. London: Arrow.

Hawkins, P. and Shohet, R. (2012) *Supervision in the Helping Professions.* Maidenhead: Open University Press.

Hawkins, P. and Smith, N. (2013) *Coaching, Mentoring and Organisational Consultancy: Supervision, Skills and Development*. Maidenhead: Open University Press.

Hay, J. (2007) *Reflective Practice and Supervision for Coaches*. Maidenhead: Open University Press.

Heidegger, M. (1962) *Being and Time*. Oxford: Blackwell.

Heimann, P. (1950) 'On counter-transference', *International Journal of Psycho-Analysis*, 31: 81–4.

Hirschhorn, L. (1990) *The Workplace Within: Psychodynamics of Organizational Life*. Cambridge, MA: MIT Press.

Hubble, M., Duncan, B., & Miller, S. (1999) *The Heart and Soul of Change: What Works in Therapy*. Washington, DC: American Psychological Association.

Kadushin, A. (1976) *Supervision in Social Work*. New York: Columbia University Press.

Kegan, R. and Lahey, L. (2009) *Immunity to Change*. Boston, MA: Harvard Business School Press.

Kline, N. (2009) *More Time to Think: A Way of Being in the World*. Otley: Fisher King Publications.

Knights, A. (2008) *Developing Coaching Capability in Organisations*. London: Chartered Institute of Personnel and Development.

Lambert, M. and Ogles, B. (2004) 'The efficacy and effectiveness of psychotherapy', in Lambert, M. (ed.), *Bergin and Garfield's Handbook of Psychotherapy and Behavior Change* (5th edn). Chicago, IL: John Wiley and Sons, pp. 139–93.

Lapworth, P. and Sills, C. (2011) *An Introduction to Transactional Analysis*. London: Sage.

Lee, G. (2003) *Leadership Coaching: From Personal Insight to Organisational Excellence*. London: Chartered Institute of Personnel and Development.

Lewin, K. (1952) *Field Theory in Social Science: Selected Theoretical Papers*. London: Tavistock.

Lietaer, G. (1993) 'Authenticity, congruence and transparency', in D. Brazier (ed.), *Beyond Carl Rogers*. London: Constable, pp. 17–46. Available at www.elementsuk.com/libraryofarticles/authenticity.pdf (accessed March 2015).

Little, M. (1951) 'Countertransference and the patient's response to it', *International Journal of Psycho-Analysis*, 32: 32–40.

Livermore, D. (2010) *Leading with Cultural Intelligence*. New York: American Management Association.

Luborsky, L., Singer, B. and Luborsky, L. (1975) 'Comparative studies of psychotherapies: is it true that "Everyone has won and all must have prizes"?', *Archives of General Psychiatry*, 32: 995–1008.

Luborsky, L., Diguer, L., Seligman, D., Rosenthal, R., Krause, E., Johnson, S. et al. (1999) 'The researcher's own therapy allegiances: a "wild card" in comparisons of treatment efficacy', *Clinical Psychology: Science and Practice*, 6(1): 95–106.

Malan, D. (1999) *Individual Psychotherapy and the Science of Psychodynamics*. Oxford: Butterworth-Heinemann.

McKee, A., Boyatzis, R. and Johnston, F. (2008) *Becoming a Resonant Leader: Develop Your Emotional Intelligence, Renew Your Relationships, Sustain Your Effectiveness*. Boston, MA: Harvard Business School Press.

McKenna, D. and Davis, S. (2009) 'Hidden in plain sight: the active ingredients of executive coaching', *Industrial and Organisational Psychology: Perspectives on Science and Practice*, 2: 244–60.

Menzies Lyth, I. ([1970] 1988) 'The functioning of social systems as a defence against anxiety', in I. Menzies Lyth, *Containing Anxiety in Institutions: Selected Essays* (vol. 1). London: Free Association Books.

Mitchell, S. (1988) *Relational Concepts in Psychoanalysis: An Integration*. Cambridge, MA: Harvard University Press.

Mitchell, S. (2000) *Relationality: From Attachment to Intersubjectivity*. Hillsdale, NJ: The Analytic Press.

Moerman, D. (2002) *Meaning, Medicine and the 'Placebo Effect'*. Cambridge: Cambridge University Press.

Murdoch, E. (2008) *Virtual Coach and Mentor Supervision*. Available at: http://coaching supervisionacademy.com/thought-leadership/virtual-coach-mentor-sup-em/ (accessed March 2015).

Nagel, T. (1989) *The View from Nowhere*. Oxford: Oxford University Press.

Nevis, E. (1997) *Organizational Consulting: A Gestalt Approach*. Cambridge, MA: Gestalt Press.

Norcross, J., Levant, R. and Beutler, L. (2006) *Evidence-Based Practices in Mental Health: Debate and Dialogue on the Fundamental Questions*. Washington, DC: American Psychological Association.

O'Connor, J. and Lages, A. (2007) *How Coaching Works: The Essential Guide to the History and Practice of Effective Coaching*. London: A & C Black.

O'Neill, M.B. (2007) *Executive Coaching with Backbone and Heart: A Systems Approach to Engaging Leaders with their Challenges*. New York: John Wiley and Sons.

Orlinsky, D., Ronnestad, M. and Willutzki, U. (2004) 'Fifty years of psychotherapy process-outcome research: continuity and change', in Lambert, M. (ed.), *Bergin and Garfield's Handbook of Psychotherapy and Behavior Change* (5th edn). Chicago, IL: John Wiley and Sons, pp. 307–89.

Oshry, B. (1999) *Leading Systems: Lessons from the Power Lab*. San Francisco, CA: Berrett-Koehler.

Palmer, S. and Whybrow, A. (2007) *Handbook of Coaching Psychology: A Guide for Practitioners*. Hove: Routledge.

Parlett, M. (1991) 'Reflections on field theory', *British Gestalt Journal*, 1: 68–9.

Parlett, M. (1997) 'The unified field in practice', *Gestalt Review*, 1(1): 16–33.

Parsloe, E. (1999) *The Manager as Coach and Mentor*. London: Chartered Institute of Personnel and Development.

Pascal, B. (1995) *Pensees*. London: Penguin Classics.

Passmore, J. (ed.) (2013) *Diversity in Coaching: Working with Gender, Culture, Race and Age*. London: Kogan Page.

Passmore, J. and Fillery-Travis, A. (2011) 'A critical review of executive coaching research: a decade of progress and what's to come', *Coaching: An International Journal of Theory, Research and Practice*, 4(2): 70–88.

Paul, S. and Pelham, G. (2000) 'A relational approach to therapy', in S. Palmer and R. Woolfe (eds), *Integrative and Eclectic Counselling and Psychotherapy*. London: Sage, pp. 110–26.

Pearsall, J. (ed.) (1999) *The Concise Oxford Dictionary*. Oxford: Oxford University Press.

Pelham, G. (1982) *A Critical Analysis of the Work of B.F. Skinner*. PhD thesis, University of Bradford.

Pelham, G. (2008) 'The relational approach', in S. Haugh and S. Paul (eds), *The Therapeutic Relationship: Perspectives and Themes*. Ross-on-Wye: PCCS Books.

Pelham, G. (2014) 'Not just personal: the meaning of moods', *Coaching Today: The Journal of BACP Coaching*, April 2014.

Pelham, G., Paul, S. and Holmes, P. (1996) 'A relational model of counselling in counselling', *Journal of the British Association for Counselling*, 7(3): 229–31.

Peterson, B. (2004) *Cultural Intelligence: A Guide to Working with People from Other Cultures*. Yarmouth, ME: Intercultural Press.

Pitt-Aikens, T. and Thomas Ellis, A. (1990) *Loss of the Good Authority: Cause of Delinquency*. London: Penguin Books.

Polanyi, M. (2009) *The Tacit Dimension*. Chicago, IL: University of Chicago Press.

Prochaska, J., Norcross, J. and DiClemente, C. (1998) *Changing for Good*. New York: Avon Books.

Proctor, B. (1988) 'Supervision: a co-operative exercise in accountability', in N. Marken and M. Payne (eds), *Enabling and Ensuring*. Leicester: National Youth Bureau and Council for Education and Training in Youth and Community Work.

Rainey Tolbert, M.A. and Hanafin, J. (2006) 'Use of self in OD consulting: what matters is presence', in B. Jones and M. Brazzel (eds), *The NTL Handbook of Organization Development and Change: Principles, Practices, and Perspectives*. New York: John Wiley and Sons, pp. 69–82.

Ridler & Co (2013) *The Ridler Report*. Available at: www.ridlerandco.com/ridler-report/ (accessed April 2015).

Rogers, C.R. (2003) *Client-Centred Therapy*. London: Constable.

Rogers, J. (2012) *Coaching Skills: A Handbook*. Maidenhead: Open University Press.

Rosenthal, R. and Jacobson, L. (1968) *Pygmalion in the Classroom: Teacher Expectation and Pupils' Intellectual Development*. New York: Holt, Rinehart and Winston.

Rosinski, P. (2003) *Coaching Across Cultures: New Tools for Leveraging National, Corporate and Professional Differences*. London: Nicholas Brealey.

Rowan, J. and Jacobs, J. (2002) *The Therapist's Use of Self*. Buckingham: Open University Press.

Rowland, N. and Goss, S. (2000) *Evidence-Based Counselling and Psychological Therapies*. London: Routledge.

Salovey, P. and Mayer, J.D. (1990) 'Emotional intelligence', *Imagination, Cognition, and Personality*, 9: 185–211.

Sandler, C. (2011) *Executive Coaching: A Psychodynamic Approach*. Maidenhead: Open University Press.

Satir, V. (1993) *Conjoint Family Therapy*. Palo Alto, CA: Science and Behavior Books.

Scovern, A. (1999) 'From placebo to alliance: the role of common factors in medicine', in M. Hubble, B. Duncan and S. Miller (eds), *The Heart and Soul of Change: What Works in Therapy*. Washington, DC: American Psychological Association.

Shainberg, D. (1983) 'Teaching therapists how to be with their coachees', in J. Westwood (ed.), *Awakening the Heart*. Boston, MA: Shambhala.

Sills, C. (2012) 'The coaching contract: a mutual commitment', in E. de Haan and C. Sills (eds), *Coaching Relationships: The Relational Coaching Fieldbook*. Farington: Libri.

Skiffington, S. and Zeus, P. (2000) *The Complete Guide to Coaching at Work*. London: McGraw-Hill Professional.

Snyder, C., Scott, M. and Cheavens, J. (1999) 'Hope as a psychotherapeutic foundation of common factors, placebos and expectancies', in M. Hubble, B. Duncan and S. Miller (eds), *The Heart and Soul of Change: What Works in Therapy*. Washington, DC: American Psychological Association.

St John-Brooks, K. (2013) *Internal Coaching: The Inside Story*. London: Karnac.

Stern, D. (1985) *The Interpersonal World of the Infant: A View from Psychoanalysis and Development Psychology*. London: Karnac.

Stone, H. (1993) *Embracing Your Inner Critic: Turning Self-Criticism into a Creative Asset*. New York: HarperOne.

Storolow, R. (2011) *World, Affectivity, Trauma: Heidegger and Post-Cartesian Psychoanalysis*. New York: Routledge.

Szasz, T. (1963) 'The concept of transference', *International Journal of Psycho-Analysis*, 44: 432–43.

Taylor, C. (1992) *The Ethics of Authenticity*. Cambridge, MA: Harvard University Press.

Trompenaars, F. and Hampden-Turner, C. (2012) *Riding the Waves of Culture: Understanding Cultural Diversity in Business*. London: Nicholas Brealey.

Wampold, B. and Imel, Z. (2001) *The Great Psychotherapy Debate: Models, Methods, and Findings*. New York: Routledge.

Westen, D., Novotny, C. and Thompson-Brenner, H. (2004) 'The empirical status of empirically supported psychotherapies: assumptions, findings, and reporting in controlled clinical trials', *Psychological Bulletin*, 130(4): 631–3.

Whitmore, J. (2009) *Coaching for Performance*. London: Nicholas Brealey.

Whitmore, J., Blakey, J. and Day, I. (2009) *Where Were All the Coaches When the Banks Went Down? Advanced Skills for High Performance Coaching*. Shirley: 121 Partners Ltd.

Whittington, J. (2012) *Systemic Coaching and Constellations*. London: Kogan Page.

Wildflower, L. (2013) *The Hidden History of Coaching*. Maidenhead: Open University Press.

Williams, R. (2014) *Keywords: A Vocabulary of Culture and Society*. London: Fourth Estate.

Wosket, V. (1999) *The Therapeutic Use of Self: Counselling Practice, Research and Supervision*. London: Routledge.

Yalom, I. (2002) *The Gift of Therapy*. London: Piatkus.

Index